Central America

Opposing Viewpoints®

Central America

Opposing Viewpoints®

David L. Bender & Bruno Leone, Series Editors

Bonnie Szumski, Book Editor
Claudia Debner, Associate Editor
Terry O'Neill, Associate Editor
Lynn Hall, Editorial Assistant
Pat Jordan, Editorial Assistant

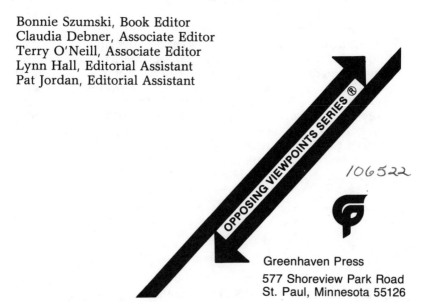

106522

Greenhaven Press
577 Shoreview Park Road
St. Paul, Minnesota 55126

Library of Congress Cataloging in Publication Data

Central America, opposing viewpoints.

(Opposing viewpoints series)
Bibliography: p.
Includes index.
1. Central America—Politics and government—1979—Addresses, essays, lectures. 2. Central America—Foreign relations—United States—Addresses, essays, lectures. 3. United States—Foreign relations—Central America—Addresses, essays, lectures. 4. Communism—Central America—Addresses, essays, lectures. I. Szumski, Bonnie, 1958- II. O'Neill, Terry, 1944- III. Debner, Claudia, 1951- IV. Series.
F1439.5.C456 1984 327.728073 84-13651
ISBN 0-89908-322-6 (pbk.)
ISBN 0-89908-347-1 (lib. bdg.)

"Congress shall make no law...
abridging the freedom of speech,
or of the press."

first amendment to the U.S. Constitution

The basic foundation of our democracy is the first amendment guarantee of freedom of expression. The *Opposing Viewpoints Series* is dedicated to the concept of this basic freedom and the idea that it is more important to practice it than to enshrine it.

Contents

Why Consider Opposing Viewpoints?

"It is better to debate a question without settling it than to settle a question without debating it."

Joseph Joubert (1754-1824)

The Importance of Examining Opposing Viewpoints

The purpose of the Opposing Viewpoints Series, and this book in particular, is to present balanced, and often difficult to find, opposing points of view on complex and sensitive issues.

Probably the best way to become informed is to analyze the positions of those who are regarded as experts and well studied on issues. It is important to consider every variety of opinion in an attempt to determine the truth. Opinions from the mainstream of society should be examined. But also important are opinions that are considered radical, reactionary, or minority as well as those stigmatized by some other uncomplimentary label. An important lesson of history is the eventual acceptance of many unpopular and even despised opinions. The ideas of Socrates, Jesus, and Galileo are good examples of this.

Readers will approach this book with their own opinions on the issues debated within it. However, to have a good grasp of one's own viewpoint, it is necessary to understand the arguments of those with whom one disagrees. It can be said that those who do not completely understand their adversary's point of view do not fully understand their own.

A persuasive case for considering opposing viewpoints has been presented by John Stuart Mill in his work *On Liberty*. When examining controversial issues it may be helpful to reflect on his suggestion:

> The only way in which a human being can make some approach to knowing the whole of a subject, is by hearing what can be said about it by persons of every variety of opinion, and studying all modes in which it can be looked at by every character of mind. No wise man ever acquired his wisdom in any mode but this.

Analyzing Sources of Information

The Opposing Viewpoints Series includes diverse materials taken from magazines, journals, books, and newspapers, as well as statements and position papers from a wide range of individuals, organizations and governments. This broad spectrum of sources helps to develop patterns of thinking which are open to the consideration of a variety of opinions.

Pitfalls to Avoid

A pitfall to avoid in considering opposing points of view is that of regarding one's own opinion as being common sense and the most rational stance and the point of view of others as being only opinion and naturally wrong. It may be that another's opinion is correct and one's own is in error.

Another pitfall to avoid is that of closing one's mind to the opinions of those with whom one disagrees. The best way to approach a dialogue is to make one's primary purpose that of understanding the mind and arguments of the other person and not that of enlightening him or her with one's own solutions. More can be learned by listening than speaking.

It is my hope that after reading this book the reader will have a deeper understanding of the issues debated and will appreciate the complexity of even seemingly simple issues on which good and honest people disagree. This awareness is particularly important in a democratic society such as ours where people enter into public debate to determine the common good. Those with whom one disagrees should not necessarily be regarded as enemies, but perhaps simply as people who suggest different paths to a common goal.

Developing Basic Reading and Thinking Skills

In this book carefully edited opposing viewpoints are purposely placed back to back to create a running debate; each viewpoint is preceded by a short quotation that best expresses the author's main argument. This format instantly plunges the reader into the midst of a controversial issue and greatly aids that reader in mastering the basic skill of recognizing an author's point of view.

A number of basic skills for critical thinking are practiced in the activities that appear throughout the books in the series. Some of the skills are:

Evaluating Sources of Information The ability to choose from among alternative sources the most reliable and accurate source in relation to a given subject.

Separating Fact from Opinion The ability to make the basic distinction between factual statements (those that can be demonstrated or verified empirically) and statements of opinion (those that are beliefs or attitudes that cannot be proved).

Identifying Stereotypes The ability to identify oversimplified, exaggerated descriptions (favorable or unfavorable) about people and insulting statements about racial, religious or national groups, based upon misinformation or lack of information.

Recognizing Ethnocentrism The ability to recognize attitudes or opinions that express the view that one's own race, culture, or group is inherently superior, or those attitudes that judge another culture or group in terms of one's own.

It is important to consider opposing viewpoints and equally important to be able to critically analyze those viewpoints. The activities in this book are designed to help the reader master these thinking skills. Statements are taken from the book's viewpoints and the reader is asked to analyze them. This technique aids the reader in developing skills that not only can be applied to the viewpoints in this book, but also to situations where opinionated spokespersons comment on controversial issues. Although the activities are helpful to the solitary reader, they are most useful when the reader can benefit from the interaction of group discussion.

Using this book and others in the series should help readers develop basic reading and thinking skills. These skills should improve the reader's ability to understand what they read. Readers should be better able to separate fact from opinion, substance from rhetoric and become better consumers of information in our media-centered culture.

This volume of the Opposing Viewpoints Series does not advocate a particular point of view. Quite the contrary! The very nature of the book leaves it to the reader to formulate the opinions he or she find most suitable. My purpose as publisher is to see that this is made possible by offering a wide range of viewpoints which are fairly presented.

David L. Bender
Publisher

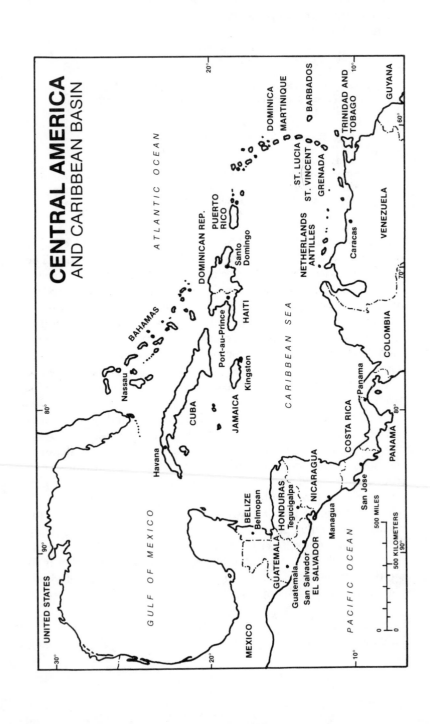

CENTRAL AMERICA
AND CARIBBEAN BASIN

UNITED STATES

GULF OF MEXICO

ATLANTIC OCEAN

BAHAMAS

Nassau

Havana

CUBA

MEXICO

JAMAICA

Kingston

Port-au-Prince

HAITI

DOMINICAN REP.

Santo Domingo

PUERTO RICO

CARIBBEAN SEA

DOMINICA

MARTINIQUE

ST. LUCIA

ST. VINCENT

GRENADA

BARBADOS

TRINIDAD AND TOBAGO

NETHERLANDS ANTILLES

Caracas

VENEZUELA

GUYANA

COLOMBIA

BELIZE

Belmopan

GUATEMALA

Guatemala

San Salvador

EL SALVADOR

HONDURAS

Tegucigalpa

NICARAGUA

Managua

COSTA RICA

San Jose

Panama

PANAMA

PACIFIC OCEAN

500 MILES

500 KILOMETERS

0

30°

20°

10°

20°

10°

90°

80°

70°

60°

Introduction

"The American continents. . .should consider any attempt on [Europe's] part to extend their system to any portion of this hemisphere as dangerous to our peace and safety."

The Monroe Doctrine, December 2, 1823

In the heated debate over Central America, one question frequently arises: Why should the political affairs of a militarily weak, poverty-stricken cluster of nations be deemed of "strategic interest" to the United States? The answer lies in the fact that a superpower like the US considers nations in its hemisphere as being within its "sphere of influence." Consequently, it is believed that any radical social, economic, or political changes within adjacent regions may affect the national security and/or prestige of the United States.

The US is certainly not the only nation holding this geopolitical worldview. Following the Soviet invasion of Czechoslovakia in 1968, Soviet Premier Leonid Brezhnev said that the USSR would intervene in the domestic affairs of any Soviet bloc nation if Communist rule were threatened. Essentially, the so-called "Brezhnev Doctrine" was a statement affirming Eastern Europe as being within the Soviet sphere of influence. Implied was the belief that any threat to Marxist rule in Soviet-bloc nations was a direct threat to Soviet security.

Many claim that any intervention by a superpower in the affairs of sister nations can never be justified; that alleged threats to domestic security are often thin excuses for unwarranted and blatant "bullyism;" and that revolution in one state is an internal affair and should remain such. Others argue that historically, political revolution and/or social upheaval are frequently generated by political and philosophical zealots whose commitment to their ideals compel them to export their revolutions. Thus, nations neighboring these revolutionary areas should place self-interest and self-protection above all other considerations. The current situation in Central America addresses itself to these respective arguments. Indeed, Central America is one of the most crucial and problematic issues facing US foreign policy strategists since the Vietnam era.

The questions debated in this anthology of opposing viewpoints relate to US national security, the practicability and morality of US involvement in Central America, and the possibilities for peace in the region. Thoughtful viewpoints are to be found on all sides of the political spectrum, each offering compelling arguments for or against US involvement in Central America. It is essential that the reader of this book understand that the issue of Central America, as with all foreign policy issues, does not lend itself to simplistic, formulaic resolutions. The purpose of this work is to present a balanced mixture of what are believed to be some of the most credible and original ideas on the subject. Such an approach, the editors feel, leaves the reader in the best situation to reach an informed and intelligent opinion.

Why Is the US Involved in Central America?

"We must safeguard democracy and stability in our immediate neighborhood."

The US Is Promoting Democracy

George Shultz

George Shultz is the secretary of state under the Reagan administration. He has a Ph.D. from the Massachusetts Institute of Technology. During the Nixon administration he served as the secretary of labor, director of the Office of Management and Budget, and secretary of the treasury before resigning in 1974. In the following viewpoint, Secretary Shultz contends that the primary US interest in Central America is to protect democracy.

As you read, consider the following questions:

1. What three questions about Central America does Secretary Shultz address in this viewpoint?
2. What does the author believe the US should do in Central America?
3. What reasons does the author give for the US caring about what happens in Central America?

George Shultz, in an address before the Dallas World Affairs Council and Chamber of Commerce, Dallas, Texas, April 15, 1983.

I think that any discussion of Central America must address three questions.

- First of all, why should we care about Central America?
- Second, what's going on there now?
- And, third, what should we do about it?

Importance to the U.S.

The questions are important, and I'll try to answer them plainly and clearly. I think, first of all, that Central America's importance to the United States cannot be denied. Central America is so close that its troubles automatically spill over onto us; so close that the strategic posture of its countries affect ours; so close that its people's suffering brings pain to us as well.

I need not remind Texans that only the stability of our neighbors will prevent unprecedented flows of refugees northward to this country. Especially now, when a troubled world economy invites unrest, we must safeguard democracy and stability in our immediate neighborhood.

I did not use the word "strategic" lightly. Despite the 1962 Cuban missile crisis, and despite last year's war between Argentina and the United Kingdom, most Americans think of Latin America as not involved in the global strategic balance. People are aware, of course, that Cuba has intervened militarily in Africa, but they may not realize that Cuba's Army is today three times larger than it was in 1962, or that 40,000 Cuban troops are now stationed in Africa, or that 2,000 Cuban military and security advisers are in Nicaragua. Some of you may also not have noticed that Nicaragua's Minister of Defense said on April 9 that Nicaragua would consider accepting Soviet missiles if asked.

In the great debate about how best to protect our interests in the Panama Canal, the only thing all sides agreed on was that the canal is critical and must be kept open and defended. Yet the security of the Panama Canal is directly affected by the stability and security of Central America.

The canal itself is but a 50-mile span in thousands of miles of sealanes across the Caribbean. In peacetime, 44% of all foreign trade tonnage and 45% of the crude oil to the United States pass through the Caribbean. In a European war, 65% of our mobilization requirements would go by sea from gulf ports through the Florida Straits onward to Europe.

During World War II—just to remind you again—our defenses were so weak, our lifeline so exposed, that in the first months of 1942 a handful of enemy subs sank hundreds of ships in the Caribbean and the Gulf of Mexico and did it more easily and faster than did Hitler's whole fleet in the North Atlantic. The Caribbean was a better target for them. Almost exactly 41 years ago a Mexican tanker—running with full lights, as was the custom for neutrals—was sunk off Miami. That June, a single submarine, U-159, sank eight American ships in 4 days, two of them just off the entrance to the Panama Canal. Remember, Hitler's Germany had no bases in the Caribbean, not even access to ports for fuel and supplies.

Most Americans have assumed that, because the Soviet Union knows that we will not accept the emplacement of strategic weapons in Cuba, we had nothing more to fear. It's true that there are no nuclear weapons in Cuba, and it is true that Cuba's communist utopia has proved such an economic disaster that it is entirely dependent on massive Soviet aid to the tune of some $4 billion annually. Yet this has not kept Cuba from portraying itself as the vanguard of a better future and mounting a campaign to establish new communist dictatorships in Central America.

Creating and Supporting Democracy

We have an interest in creating and supporting democratic states in Central America capable of conducting their political and economic affairs free from outside interference. Strategically, we have a vital interest in not allowing the proliferation of Cuba-model states which would provide platforms for subversion, compromise vital sea lanes and pose a direct military threat at or near our borders. This would undercut us globally and create economic dislocation and a resultant influx to the U.S. of illegal immigrants. In the short run we must work to eliminate Cuban/Soviet influence in the region, and in the long run we must build politically stable governments able to withstand such influences.

National Security Council, Summary Paper, April 1982.

There are some people I know who think we in the Administration are exaggerating the danger. Let me, however, read you this quote:

> The revolutionary process of Central America is a single process. The triumphs of one are the triumphs of the other. . . . Guatemala will have its hour. Honduras its. Costa Rica, too, will have its hour of glory. The first note was heard in Nicaragua.

In case you're wondering, the speaker was not an Administration spokesman. That confident prediction comes from Cayetano Carpio, principal leader of the Salvadoran guerrillas in the August 25, 1980, edition of the Mexican magazine *Proceso*. Look it up.

Our analysis, our strategy, our predictions for the future of Central America are rooted in two perceptions. One is that democracy cannot flourish in the presence of extreme inequalities in access to land, opportunity, or justice. The second perception is that Mr. Carpio and his allies are exploiting such inequities for antidemocratic ends.

I quoted a terrorist leader because it is beliefs like his, backed by armed violence, that so concern our friends in Central America. In Costa Rica, where democracy and respect for human rights are an ancient tradtion; in Honduras, where democratic institutions are catching hold; in El Salvador, where democracy is beginning to work; even in Nicaragua, where disillusionment is the order of the day.

Ask the people who live there. They will tell you, as they have told us—through their governments, in their public opinion polls, and in their newspaper and radio editorials—that the revolution about which Carpio boasts is a frightening phenomenon: a direct threat to their democracy and well-being. They will tell you that we North Americans should also be concerned. Not because Mr. Carpio will tomorrow lead an FMLN [Farabundo Marti National Liberation Front] battalion across the Rio Grande, but because the cause of democracy and human rights is our cause too.

Frankly, I agree. We cannot in good conscience look the other way when democracy and human rights are challenged in countries very near to us, countries that look to us for help. President Reagan put it well last month: "Human rights," he said, "means working at problems, not walking away from them."

US Strategy

So the key question is: What should we do? A primary element of our strategy must be to support democracy, reform, and the protection of human rights. Democracies are far less likely to threaten their neighbors or abuse their citizens than dictatorships.

The forces of democracy are many and varied. Some are deeply rooted, as in Costa Rica, which has known nothing but democracy for 35 years. Others are more fragile but have grown steadily as economic development has strenghened the middle class and as trade unions and peasant organizations are making pluralism a reality. The Catholic Church has also made important contributions to democracy and social progress. So also has the United States through culture, example, and more recently through diplomacy as well.

The forces of dictatorship are of two kinds. One is old, the other new. The old variety is that of economic oligarchy, political despotism, and military repression. Except for Costa Rica, this has been the traditional method of social organization for most of Central America's history. The new form of dictatorship is that of a command economy, a self-appointed elitist vanguard, and guerrilla war. Nicaragua has become its base, all of Central America its target.

Before the Sandinistas came to power in Nicaragua in 1979, they promised free elections, political pluralism, and nonalignment. Today every one of these promises is being betrayed. First the Sandinistas moved to squeeze the democrats out of the governing junta; then to restrict all political opposition, all press freedom, and the independence of the church; then to build what is now the largest armed force in the history of Central America; then to align themselves with the Soviet Union and Cuba in subverting their neighbors.

El Salvador became the first target. In 1980, at Cuban direction, several Salvadoran extremist groups were unified in Managua, where their operational headquarters remains to this day. Cuba and its Soviet-bloc allies then provided training and supplies which began to flow clandestinely through Nicaragua to El Salvador to fuel an armed assault. The communist intervention has not brought guerrillas to power, but it has cost thousands of lives and widened an already bitter conflict. Today El Salvador hangs in the balance with reforming democrats pitted against the forces of old and new dictatorships alike.

The US Different from USSR

Soviet intervention occurs in support of totalitarianism, ours in order to block totalitarianism. That is an enormous difference. . . .

The same is true of revolutions: they have differing political content. Revolutions have certainly been carried out by Lenin, Mao, Hitler, Castro, and now by the Sandinistas. They are antidemocratic in content. The American and French revolutions were democratic in content, so was the Solidarity movement, and so was the revolution in China led by Sun Yat-sen, which was aborted by war and Mao.

Jeffrey Hart, *Manchester Union Leader*, August 17, 1983.

The struggle for democracy is made even more difficult by the heavy legacy of decades of social and economic inequities. And in El Salvador, as elsewhere, the world recession has hit with devastating effects.

Supporting Economic Development

We must also, therefore, support economic development. Underdevelopment, recession, and the guerrillas' "prolonged war" against El Salvador's economy cause human hardship and misery that are being cynically exploited by the enemies of democracy. Three-quarters of the funds that we are spending in support of our Central American policy go to economic assistance. And our economic program goes beyond traditional aid: The President's Caribbean Basin Initiative is meant to provide powerful trade and investment incentives to help these countries achieve self-sustaining economic growth.

But just as no amount of reform can bring peace so long as guerrillas believe they can win a military victory, no amount of economic help will suffice if guerrilla units can destroy roads, bridges, power stations, and crops again and again with impunity. So we must also support the security of El Salvador and the other threatened nations of the region.

Finally, faced with a grave regionwide crisis, we must seek regional, peaceful solutions. We are trying to persuade the Sandinistas that they should come to the bargaining table, ready to come to terms with their neighbors and with their own increasingly troubled society. . . .

Commitment to Democracy

Our commitment to peace and democracy in Central America is not. . . limited to El Salvador and Nicaragua. Like us, Costa Rica and Honduras have not given up hope that Nicaragua will return to the tenets of democracy and peace for which its people fought in 1979. But as Nicaragua's immediate neighbor, they feel directly the spillover of Nicaragua's militarization and growing internal troubles. Six thousand Nicaraguans are now living in exile in Costa Rica. In Honduras the flow of refugees from Nicaragua continues to rise. Last year alone, some 15,000 Miskito Indians fled to Honduras rather than accept forced relocation by the Nicaraguan Government.

Until a peaceful solution is found, we must continue to bolster Honduras and Costa Rica. Both are democratic. Both have been hit hard economically by the regional turmoil and the world recession. And both have been victimized by terrorism directed from Nicaragua. We want to strengthen these democracies and help them provide their people stability and hope, even in the midst of regional crisis.

Democracy in Central America will not be achieved overnight, and it will not be achieved without sustained U.S. support. To support our objectives in Central America—democracy development, justice, and the security to make them possible—Congress has authorized substantial economic assistance. Controversy continues, however, over military aid to El Salvador—the country literally under the gun.

The security assistance we have asked for is to build disciplined, skilled armed forces to serve as a shield for democratization and development—a shield. We are not planning to Americanize the fighting or to send El Salvador advanced, heavy weapons, like Nicaragua's Soviet tanks. We will help El

21

Salvador's Armed Forces to increase their mobility and to acquire necessary munitions, spare parts, engineering equipment, and medical supplies. But our primary emphasis is on greatly expanded training for Salvadoran soldiers. As I mentioned earlier, only a tenth of the soldiers have received our training, and those who have, have a superior performance. So if we can increase that level of training, we can expect performance to improve.

Time is important. To quote Senator Henry Jackson, "If you're going to have the ballot box free and open, there must be a shield behind which the people can participate." Whether we will be able to help provide this shield in time depends on the Congress. In the middle of a war, the Congress has cut security assistance to a level two-thirds below the previous fiscal year. So here you are—you're an army, you're fighting—and all of a sudden the flow of what you need to fight with is cut by two-thirds. Then people ask, "How come that army isn't doing better?" It's a terrific blow.

The Administration is seeking to restore these funds. The people of El Salvador must have confidence that we will see their struggle through, or else hope for democracy may not survive.

Reasons for US Involvement

In summation, let me say again that there are many reasons for us to care about what happens in Central America. One is strategic, and we better remember it. What is happening in Central America could endanger our own security and that of our friends throughout the Caribbean Basin, from Mexico to the Panama Canal.

But an equal reason is moral. How can we, in the name of human rights, abandon our neighbors to a brutal, military takeover by a totalitarian minority? If our concern is freedom, will a communist victory provide it? If our concern is judicial fairness, will a communist regime provide it? If our concern is poverty, will a communist economic system provide prosperity?

The American people and their elected representatives have difficult choices to make. It is easy to play the demagogue, and it is tempting to avoid hard decisions. But if we walk away from this challenge, we will have let down not only all those in Central America who yearn for democracy, but we will have let ourselves down. We cannot be for freedom and human rights only in the abstract. If our ideals are to have meaning, we must defend them when they are threatened. Let us meet our responsibility.

"Our stated aim of promoting democracy implies that some of our Latin American friends must run elections once in a while."

The US Is Not Promoting Democracy

Francis Chamberlain

Francis Chamberlain S. J., an American Jesuit, has been serving in Lima, Peru since 1969. In the following viewpoint, Father Chamberlain contends that the US backs repressive regimes that bolster US economic aims rather than support democracy in Central America.

As you read, consider the following questions:

1. Does the author believe that "there is a long-standing pattern of American support" for repressive regimes? What evidence does he give?
2. What does the author believe are America's real interests in Central America?
3. Why is it important to question what United States officials mean when they speak about "democracy," according to the author?

Francis Chamberlain, "Six Unanswered Questions About Latin America," *America*, February 25, 1984. Reprinted with permission of America Press, Inc., 106 West 56th Street, New York, NY 10019.

My 15 years in Latin America have led me to believe that not all the questions about U.S. policy are being asked, let alone being answered. I would like, then, to share these questions,. . .in the hope that they may contribute to the needed national debate.

Is there a long-standing pattern of American support, whether direct or indirect, for systematic, institutionalized terror, torture and murder in Latin America?

Such a question, especially in its formulation, may well "turn off" many people. If the question were: "Has the United States been guilty of supporting right-wing governments in Latin America?" it might be more readily accepted. We think we understand what "right-wing" means: It conjures up images of Jerry Falwell and Senator Jesse Helms (R., N.C.). But the truth is that when the term "right-wing" is applied to governments in Latin America we are not referring to the likes of Senator Helms and the Moral Majority. We are talking about the systematic suppression of organized dissent, a suppression that is based on institutionalized terror, torture and murder. This is the case of the 40-year rule of the Somozas in Nicaragua, Guatemala since the overthrow of the democratic government of Jacobo Arbenz in 1954, the generals in Argentina after the overthrow of Isabel Perón, the Pinochet regime in Chile, Banzer's in Bolivia, the military government in Brazil since 1964, Uruguay under the army with its civilian puppets. All of these governments, and my list is incomplete, have been "friendly" toward the United States. All have received substantial military aid and training for their military and police forces. All have been helped by the I.M.F., the Inter-American Development Bank and other international lending agencies over which the United States has a decisive influence. Yet all these governments have institutionalized terror as a means of staying in power.

The point is not to detail the horror story of recent Latin American history, but to suggest that in the last 30 years in Latin America there has been a pattern of growing, institutionalized violence by governments friendly to and supported by the United States. Does the United States have any responsibility for this institutionalized violence? Why is the suppression of human rights in Poland so worthy of condemnation while the mass terror of friendly governments in Latin America is not? The question of long-standing support of terror, torture and murder is a hard question because it implies that we may have a heavy share of responsibility for the deaths of literally tens of thousands of men and women in Latin America. But the question should not, must not be avoided. A respect for the dead and a hope for the living demand that the question be taken seriously.

What are U.S. interests in Latin America?. . .

The intent of U.S. policy for at least the past 30 years has been

Ben Sargent, *The Austin American Statesman,* reprinted with permission.

to create and support client regimes—governments committed to our understanding of the world struggle between freedom and totalitarianism, between free enterprise and collectivism. Those governments open to free and untrammeled foreign, private investment have been considered "good" and on the side of freedom in the world struggle against Communism. There has been some recognition that these good governments, friendly to our interests, have for the most part been military dictatorships of the right, allied with elitist elements of the native society. There has been much less willingness to recognize that these dictatorships and their elitist supporters have maintained their position of power by institutionalizing systems of mass terror over the local population. El Salvador, Guatemala, Brazil, Chile and Argentina are prime examples of such terror, although they are by no means the only ones.

The link between freedom and unrestricted foreign investment is at the heart of U.S. policy in Latin America. Those who are friends of corporate investment are friends of freedom. What is bad for corporate investment is somehow a blow against freedom. And so we support governments that put no strings on foreign investment, however repressive they may be.

Is what I am saying here about U.S. policy too simplistic?

Perhaps, but then again perhaps not. The point is that the question about our real interests in Latin America needs to be debated. What interests has our policy defended? What effects has that policy had on the local populations of Latin America? What interests should we be promoting?

The Meaning of Democracy

What do we mean by democracy?

In spite of all its shortcomings, the democratic tradition in the United States is a major achievement and is still very much alive. One does not have to accept the messianic idealism of Woodrow Wilson and his crusade to make the world safe for democracy to state that the American experience is a valid one whose best traditions and principles should guide our dealings with other countries.

Our stated aim of promoting democracy implies that some of our Latin American friends must run elections once in a while. Elections are held up as proof that they are on the road to democracy and that the United States is doing all in its power to promote the democratic cause—no matter that the spectrum of choice in these elections runs from extreme right to "moderate" groups ("moderate" is State Department jargon referring to groups that are mildly reformist at best but still basically friendly to our interests).

Elections are, of course, a factor in any truly democratic process. But it is curious that official U.S. concern for the electoral process has at best been muted in countries like Brazil, Chile, Uruguay and Paraguay. And when I say "muted," I am understating the case. Might it be that the concern for democracy and elections comes to the fore only in hot situations like El Salvador, when the old ways of doing business will no longer work? Might it be that the need for elections is directly related to the necessity of justifying the huge outlays of arms that governments like El Salvador's need to survive? Why is the concern for democracy and elections so selective?

More importantly, official U.S. propaganda identifies democracy with elections, but this identification is patently false, not only in terms of Latin American history, but in terms of U.S. experience as well. The democratic and participatory process implies other rights just as basic, and perhaps even more basic, than the right to vote in an election. The right to organize and the right to protest, the right to promote one's views are inherent rights in any truly democratic process. . . . Without the right to organize freely and protest, without the right to free expression, the mere right to vote is hollow. The democratic tradition implies much more than the simple right to vote.

The reduction of the democratic tradition to the electoral process propagates a caricature of that tradition, and this is what official U.S. propaganda tends to do, especially today in the Central American crisis. Thus the present Nicaraguan Government is undemocratic because it has not yet held elections, in spite of the fact that, with all its very real faults, a truly impressive grassroots participatory process has been initiated in that country. Thus the Government of El Salvador is on the road to democracy because of its elections last year, in spite of the fact that there is no true freedom for independent organizations, no true freedom of expression and protest—freedoms that make the electoral process meaningful. And the lack of these basic freedoms is not due to the present civil war; rather the persistent denial of these freedoms was one of the major causes for the outbreak of war.

Democracy Becomes an Excuse

By repeating lies and distortions often enough, the administration may be able to fool some U.S. workers some of the time. But lies and distortions can cover up reality for only so long. The administration's strained efforts to justify its belligerent opposition to Nicaragua despite its scheduled elections has put a crack in its facade of concern for democracy. Its hypocritical double standard for Nicaragua and El Salvador cracks the facade further. And the growing success of the rebel movement in El Salvador helps expose the administration's claim that the people in that country support the existing regime and its sick caricature of democracy.

Sooner or later, the truth will become more apparent—that the U.S. government has no regard for democracy or freedom in Central America. Nor does it act with much regard for human rights—or human life. When the veneer is stripped away, it becomes apparent that what the United States is after is political and economic control over Central America, to enrich the wealth and power of the U.S. capitalist class.

The People, March 31, 1984.

And so the need to ask the question: What do we mean by democracy? What kind of social and political process do we wish to promote and support in Latin America? What kind of foreign policy is in accord with our best democratic and participatory traditions? Such questions cannot be avoided. The United States exerts tremendous power in Latin America. That power can be on the side of oppression or on the side of true freedom. It cannot be neutral.

Are the Soviets and the Cubans behind it all?

The question is not as simple as it looks, but to ask it runs counter to official U.S. propaganda, which sees Cuba and the

Soviet Union at the bottom of social unrest in Latin America. What is at the bottom of social unrest in Latin America is nothing other than the great social and economic injustice that the majority of the population suffers. By siding with those who defend "freedom" against the Communist plot for world domination, our foreign policy has in practice come down on the side of elitist groups and against the legitimate aspirations of Latin America's poor. That last phrase may seem simplistic, but what may seem simplistic in this case happens to be true.

There are, of course, Cubans in Nicaragua, and most surely the guerrillas in El Salvador are being supplied with arms from the Soviet bloc, although it should be noted that the military aid received by the guerrillas is incomparably smaller than the military aid the United States is giving to the struggling "democratic" government of that country. The State Department has also accused the Nicaraguans of being a pipe line for arms to the guerrillas in El Salvador, even though really hard evidence for this accusation has been conspicuously lacking. But I do not wish to quibble, because I personally would be surprised if it were discovered that the Sandinistas were not helping the insurgents in El Salvador. But what are we to make of this aid and support? Does it mean that the guerrillas in El Salvador and the Sandinistas in Nicaragua are puppets of Cuba and their Russian mentors?

American Revolution as Example

Let me ask the same question in terms of our American history. The final battle of Yorktown in our revolutionary war might have turned out quite differently, were it not for the active military support of France. Did the acceptance of French aid mean that George Washington and his companions were mere puppets of French imperialism? Or did it not simply mean that in their revolutionary struggle the Americans took aid where they could get it? Might not the same logic be at work today in Central America? Certainly the fact of Cuban aid is no more proof that the Central American revolutionaries have jumped into bed with Cuba and the Soviet Union than the fact of French aid in our revolutionary war proves the subservience of the Americans to the French. Is it possible that Cuban aid is accepted out of fundamental pragmatic necessity? This last question is very important because official U.S. propaganda insists that every Soviet gun in Central America is proof of an ideological and political subordination to the designs of Soviet world domination. In the official view, left wing means Marxist, Marxist means Communist, and Communist means under Russian tutelage. It is all of a piece and therefore any leftist uprising anywhere is directed by Moscow, in Latin America through its Cuba puppet. The virtue of this view is its neatness and simplicity; it provides a ready-made understanding for all social upheaval in Latin America. Its only defect is that it is not true. . . .

The critical attitude within the Marxist movement in Latin America is not the result of some academic lucubrations, but is based on hard historical experience. It is widely accepted within the movement that the Soviet experience has not worked. Why imitate the Soviet Union when that experience has produced new forms of unfreedom and oppression? Why subordinate oneself to the Soviet Union as Cuba has done? Such questioning has been common coin within the Marxist movement in Latin America for many years.

"The national security of all the Americas is at stake in Central America."

The US Is Protecting Its National Security

Ronald Reagan

Ronald Reagan was elected president of the United States in 1980. Military intervention in Central America became a critical issue during his administration. In the following viewpoint, President Reagan explains why he believes that the conflict in Central America directly endangers our national security.

As you read, consider the following questions:

1. Why is US security threatened in Central America, according to President Reagan?
2. What are the four basic goals the President wants to pursue in Central America?
3. What assurances does the President outline in support of his goals?

Ronald Reagan, in an address before a joint session of Congress on April 27, 1983.

Central America's problems do directly affect the security and the well-being of our own people. And Central America is much closer to the United States than many of the world trouble spots that concern us. So as we work to restore our own economy, we cannot afford to lose sight of our neighbors to the south.

El Salvador is nearer to Texas than Texas is to Massachusetts. Nicaragua is just as close to Miami, San Antonio, San Diego, and Tucson as those cities are to Washington where we're gathered tonight. But nearness on the map doesn't even begin to tell the strategic importance of Central America, bordering as it does on the Caribbean—our lifeline to the outside world. Two-thirds of all our foreign trade and petroleum pass through the Panama Canal and the Caribbean. In a European crisis, at least half of our supplies for NATO would go through these areas by sea. It's well to remember that in early 1942 a handful of Hitler's submarines sank more tonnage there than in all of the Atlantic Ocean. And they did this without a single naval base anywhere in the area.

Today, the situation is different. Cuba is host to a Soviet combat brigade, a submarine base capable of servicing Soviet submarines, and military air bases visited regularly by Soviet military aircraft.

Because of its importance, the Caribbean Basin is a magnet for adventurism. We are all aware of the Libyan cargo planes refueling in Brazil a few days ago on their way to deliver medical supplies to Nicaragua. Brazilian authorities discovered the so-called medical supplies were actually munitions and prevented their delivery. You may remember that last month, speaking on national television, I showed an aerial photo of an airfield being built on the island of Grenada. Well, if that airfield had been completed, those planes could have refueled there and completed their journey.

If the Nazis during World War II and the Soviets today could recognize the Caribbean and Central America as vital to our interests, shouldn't we also?. . .

Relations with Nicaragua

Let me set the record straight on Nicaragua, a country next to El Salvador. In 1979, when the new government took over in Nicaragua, after a revolution which overthrew the authoritarian rule of Somoza, everyone hoped for the growth of democracy. We in the United States did too. By January of 1981, our emergency relief and recovery aid to Nicaragua totaled $118 million—more than provided by any other developed country. In fact, in the first 2 years of Sandinista rule, the United States directly or indirectly sent five times more aid to Nicaragua than it had in the 2 years prior to the revolution. Can anyone doubt the generosity and good faith of the American people?

31

Bill Deore, *The Dallas Morning News*, reprinted with permission.

These were hardly the actions of a nation implacably hostile to Nicaragua. Yet, the Government of Nicaragua has treated us as an enemy. It has rejected our repeated peace efforts. It has broken its promises to us, to the Organization of American States, and, most important of all, to the people of Nicaragua. . . .

The Sandinista revolution in Nicaragua turned out to be just an exchange of one set of autocratic rulers for another, and the people still have no freedom, no democratic rights, and more poverty. Even worse than its predecessor, it is helping Cuba and the Soviets to destabilize our hemisphere.

The Government of El Salvador, making every effort to guarantee democracy, free labor unions, freedom of religion, and a free press, is under attack by guerrillas dedicated to the same philosophy that prevails in Nicaragua, Cuba, and, yes, the Soviet Union. Violence has been Nicaragua's most important export to the world. It is the ultimate in hypocrisy for the unelected Nicaraguan Government to charge that we seek their overthrow when they're doing everything they can to bring down the elected Government of El Salvador. The guerrilla attacks are directed from a headquarters in Managua, the capital of Nicaragua.

But let us be clear as to the American attitude toward the Government of Nicaragua. We do not seek its overthrow. Our interest is to ensure that it does not infect its neighbors through the export of subversion and violence. Our purpose, in conformity with American and international law, is to prevent the flow of arms to El Salvador, Honduras, Guatemala, and Costa Rica. We have attempted to have a dialogue with the Government of Nicaragua, but it persists in its efforts to spread violence.

We should not—and we will not—protect the Nicaraguan Government from the anger of its own people. But we should, through diplomacy, offer an alternative. And, as Nicaragua ponders its options, we can and will—with all the resources of diplomacy—protect each country of Central America from the danger of war. Even Costa Rica, Central America's oldest and strongest democracy, a government so peaceful it doesn't even have an army, is the object of bullying and threats from Nicaragua's dictators.

Nicaragua's neighbors know that Sandinista promises of peace, nonalliance, and nonintervention have not been kept. Some 36 new military bases have been built; there were only 13 during the Somoza years. Nicaragua's new army numbers 25,000 men supported by a militia of 50,000. It is the largest army in Central America supplemented by 2,000 Cuban military and security advisers. It is equipped with the most modern weapons, dozens of Soviet-made tanks, 800 Soviet-bloc trucks, Soviet 152-MM howitzers, 100 antiaircraft guns, plus planes and helicopters. There are additional thousands of civilian advisers from Cuba, the Soviet Union, East Germany, Libya, and the PLO [Palestine Liberation Organization]. And we are attacked because we have 55 military trainers in El Salvador.

Guerrilla's Goals

The goal of the professional guerrilla movements in Central America is as simple as it is sinister—to destabilize the entire region from the Panama Canal to Mexico. If you doubt me on this point, just consider what Cayetano Carpio, the now-deceased Salvadoran guerrilla leader, said earlier this month. Carpio said that after El Salvador falls, El Salvador and Nicaragua would be "arm-in-arm and struggling for the total liberation of Central America."

Nicaragua's dictatorial junta, who themselves made war and won power operating from bases in Honduras and Costa Rica, like to pretend they are today being attacked by forces based in Honduras. The fact is, it is Nicaragua's Government that threatens Honduras, not the reverse. It is Nicaragua who has moved heavy tanks close to the border, and Nicaragua who speaks of war. It was Nicaraguan radio that announced. . .the creation of a new, unified, revolutionary coordinating board to push forward the Marxist struggle in Honduras. Nicaragua, supported by weapons and military resources provided by the communist bloc, represses its own people, refuses to make peace, and sponsors a guerrilla war against El Salvador.

Democracy Cannot Remain Passive

Are democracies required to remain passive while threats to their security and prosperity accumulate?

Must we just accept the destabilization of an entire region from the Panama Canal to Mexico on our southern border?

Must we sit by while independent nations of this hemisphere are integrated into the most aggressive empire the modern world has seen?

US National Security at Stake

Politically and morally, we cannot side with "Somocistas," comes the pacifist complaint. But did liberals object to fighting alongside Stalin in World War II? Did they object to using ex-Nazis in the cold war creation of NATO? Do they object to collaborating with a Chinese Peoples Army whose top officers got their foreign fighting experience killing Americans in Korea? Of course not. . . .

It is not Sandino or Zapata or Villa we face in Central America; nor is it a case of needing Marines to save the plantations of the United Fruit Co.

Central America is the hemispheric base of the successor criminal empire to Hitler's; for them the last domino is not Mexico; it is the United States.

Patrick Buchanan, *The Washington Times,* December 9, 1983.

Must we wait while Central Americans are driven from their homes, like the more than 4 million who have sought refuge out of Afghanistan or the 1.5 million who have fled Indochina or the more than 1 million Cubans who have fled Castro's Caribbean utopia? Must we, by default, leave the people of El Salvador no choice but to flee their homes, creating another tragic human exodus?

I do not believe there is a majority in the Congress or the country that counsels passivity, resignation, defeatism in the face of this challenge to freedom and security in our hemisphere.

I do not believe that a majority of the Congress or the country is prepared to stand by passively while the people of Central America are delivered to totalitarianism, and we ourselves are left vulnerable to new dangers. . . .

34

Let me say to those who invoke the memory of Vietnam: There is no thought of sending American combat troops to Central America; they are not needed—indeed, they have not been requested there. All our neighbors ask of us is assistance in training and arms to protect themselves while they build a better, freer life.

We must continue to encourage peace among the nations of Central America. We must support the regional efforts now underway to promote solutions to regional problems. We cannot be certain that the Marxist-Leninist bands who believe war is an instrument of politics will be readily discouraged. It's crucial that we not become discouraged before they do. Otherwise, the region's freedom will be lost and our security damaged in ways that can hardly be calculated.

If Central America were to fall, what would the consequences be for our position in Asia, Europe, and for alliances such as NATO? If the United States cannot respond to a threat near our own borders, why should Europeans or Asians believe that we are seriously concerned about threats to them? If the Soviets can assume that nothing short of an actual attack on the United States will provoke an American response, which ally, which friend will trust us then?

Democracy and Dictatorship

The Congress shares both the power and the responsibility for our foreign policy. Tonight, I ask you, the Congress, to join me in a bold, generous approach to the problems of peace and poverty, democracy and dictatorship in the region. Join me in a program that prevents communist victory in the short run but goes beyond to produce, for the deprived people of the area, the reality of present progress and the promise of more to come.

Let us lay the foundation for a bipartisan approach to sustain the independence and freedom of the countries of Central America. We in the Administration reach out to you in this spirit.

We will pursue four basic goals in Central America.

First. In response to decades of inequity and indifference, we will support democracy, reform, and human freedom. This means using our assistance, our powers of persuasion, and our legitimate "leverage" to bolster humane democratic systems where they already exist and to help countries on their way to that goal complete the process as quickly as human institutions can be changed. Elections—in El Salvador and also in Nicaragua—must be open to all, fair and safe. The international community must help. We will work at human rights problems, not walk away from them.

Second. In response to the challenge of world recession and, in the case of El Salvador, to the unrelenting campaign of

35

economic sabotage by the guerrillas, we will support economic development. By a margin of two-to-one, our aid is economic now, not military. Seventy-seven cents out of every dollar we will spend in the area this year goes for food, fertilizers, and other essentials for economic growth and development. And our economic program goes beyond traditional aid: The Caribbean initiative introduced in the House earlier today will provide powerful trade and investment incentives to help these countries achieve self-sustaining economic growth without exporting U.S. jobs. Our goal must be to focus our immense and growing technology to enhance health care, agriculture, and industry and to ensure that we, who inhabit this interdependent region, come to know and understand each other better, retaining our diverse identities, respecting our diverse traditions and institutions.

Building Democracy in Central America

The situation in the Caribbean-Central America region is obviously different. Preventing Soviet Cuban military dominance in this region is easier than it would have been, say, in Czechoslovakia in 1948. But if we deny arms, ammunition, and money to those fighting the Cuban-backed forces; if our European allies and United States banks keep sending more money to Nicaragua than to El Salvador; if we force those who wish to build democracy to share power with those bent on destroying it; if we simply wash our hands of the conflict; then the military strength that the Soviets and Cubans have assembled in the region is quite adequate to turn Central America into another Eastern Europe.

Fred C. Ikle, *Defense*, July 1983.

Third. In response to the military challenge from Cuba and Nicaragua—to their deliberate use of force to spread tyranny—we will support the security of the region's threatened nations. We do not view security assistance as an end in itself but as a shield for democratization, economic development, and diplomacy. No amount of reform will bring peace so long as guerrillas believe they will win by force. No amount of economic help will suffice if guerrilla units can destroy roads and bridges and power stations and crops again and again with impunity. But, with better training and material help, our neighbors can hold off the guerrillas and give democratic reform time to take root.

Fourth. We will support dialogue and negotiations—both among the countries of the region and within each country. The terms and conditions of participation in elections are negotiable. Costa Rica is a shining example of democracy. Honduras has made the move from military rule to democratic government. Guatemala is pledged to the same course. The United States will work toward a political solution in Central America which will serve the interests of the democratic process.

To support these diplomatic goals, I offer these assurances:

• The United States will support any agreement among Central American countries for the withdrawal—under fully verifiable and reciprocal conditions—of all foreign military and security advisers and troops.

• We want to help opposition groups join the political process in all countries and compete by ballots instead of bullets.

• We will support any verifiable, reciprocal agreement among Central American countries on the renunciation of support for insurgencies on neighbors' territory.

• And, finally, we desire to help Central America end its costly arms race and will support any verifiable, reciprocal agreements on the nonimportation of offensive weapons. . . .

National Security at Stake

What the Administration is asking for on behalf of freedom in Central America is so small, so minimal, considering what is at stake. The total amount requested for aid to all of Central America in 1984 is about $600 million; that's less than one-tenth of what Americans will spend this year on coin-operated video games.

In summation, I say to you that tonight there can be no question: The national security of all the Americas is at stake in Cental America. If we cannot defend ourselves there, we cannot expect to prevail elsewhere. Our credibility would collapse, our alliances would crumble, and the safety of our homeland would be put at jeopardy.

We have a vital interest, a moral duty, and a solemn responsibility. This is not a partisan issue. It is a question of our meeting our moral responsibility to ourselves, our friends, and our posterity. It is a duty that falls on all of us—the President, the Congress, and the people. We must perform it together. Who among us would wish to bear responsibility for failing to meet our shared obligation?

4

*"The emergence of a hostile regime is primarily a regional problem affecting **important** US interests, but it isn't one that. . .threatens **vital** interests."*

The US National Security Threat Is Exaggerated

Robert A. Pastor

Robert A. Pastor is a faculty research associate at the School of Public Affairs at the University of Maryland. He served as senior staff member responsible for Latin American and Caribbean affairs on the National Security Council from 1977 to 1981. In the following viewpoint, Mr. Pastor argues that the government exaggerates the security threat posed by a Marxist regime in Central America. This is an edited version of a longer article published in the July 1982 issue of *The Atlantic Monthly* which includes an in-depth section on alternative policies toward Central America. The editors of this anthology recommend that the article be read in its entirety.

As you read, consider the following questions:

1. What points does the author think need to be considered when formulating a strategy in Central America?
2. Does the author believe the US can bring political stability to Central America? Why or why not?

Robert A. Pastor, "Our Real Interests in Central America," originally published in *The Atlantic Monthly*, July 1982. Revised in 1984 by the author. Reprinted with permission of the author.

The explanations that President Reagan has offered for his policies in Central America certainly have the ring of history. "Make no mistake," Reagan said, "the well-being and security of our neighbors in this region are in our own vital interest." Why? "The Caribbean region is a vital strategic and commercial artery for the United States. Nearly half of U.S. trade, two thirds of our imported oil, and over half of our imported strategic minerals pass through the Panama Canal or the Gulf of Mexico." In the words of William Middendorf, the U.S. ambassador to the Organization of American States, the region is "right on our strategic doorstep." Middendorf argues that we should quit referring to the region as "in our own back yard"; instead, we should think of it as "our strategic front yard." In addition, the U.S. has economic and ideological interests, defined positively as a concern for freedom and democracy, or negatively as anti-communism. These answers have sustained U.S. engagement in the region since the turn of the century, but they are no longer convincing.

Merely to list these interests is to understand why the Reagan Administration has been having so much difficulty persuading the American people that a decisive battle is being fought in Central America. A "vital interest" is presumably one for which the U.S. is willing to fight. In 1914, the U.S. occupied the port of Veracruz, Mexico, to gain respect for the American flag. In 1916, the U.S. fought to ensure that customs taxes would be collected in the Dominican Republic. In 1927, U.S. troops died to ensure a free election in Nicaragua. Not only would few Americans consider any of these interests vital today but it would be hard to identify a consensus in the U.S. around *any* interest that would justify unilateral U.S. military intervention in Central America; in a 1982 poll published by the *Washington Post*, 70 percent of Americans said they would oppose any fighting by the U.S. in El Salvador.

Our interests are not immutable; they have changed as the world and our capabilities have changed. Moreover, new administrations often attach very different weights to each interest; to see this, one need only compare the importance that the past three administrations have given to U.S. national interests in human rights abroad.

There is no better example of the changing character of U.S. interests and the implications of the change for U.S. strategy than the Panama Canal, which has been the symbol of U.S. interests in Central America since the turn of the century. Even today, there are many who believe that the principal reason for preventing instability in the rest of Central America is that the Canal must be protected, lest a hostile neighbor interfere with its traffic. Through World Wars I and II, the Canal was an invaluable strategic asset, but with the advent of aircraft carriers, which were too large to pass through the Canal, U.S. interests in it changed—from strategic to primarily economic, from facilitating the movement of the U.S. fleet to providing a marginal economic advantage in the shipment of supplies. U.S. interests in an open and efficient Canal remained important, but they could hardly be considered either vital or strategic. At the same time, the Canal became vital for countries such as Panama, Ecuador, Colombia, Nicaragua, and Costa Rica, which shipped much larger percentages of their trade throught it. Closure would only marginally affect the U.S.; it would be catastrophic for these countries. The new Canal treaties between the U.S. and Panama ratified in 1978 reflected these changing interests and the necessity of a new approach to protect these interests.

National Security Risk a Myth

When politicians or officials talk of "vital interests," what they usually have in mind is money. When they say that a given Soviet action will pose "grave challenges," they mean that the United States will have to spend more dollars to counter it. They should be required to specify what they think the cost might be. Cost estimates—and whether or not they should be paid—are debatable. "Vital interests" and "grave challenges" are not. . . .

The overwhelming military advantage the United States would enjoy in its own backyard is what makes it so untenable to argue that a Soviet or Cuban presence in Central America would seriously threaten U.S. security. And it makes it likely that, if Soviet or Cuban bases ever were established in Central America, they would be used only to defend the country in which they were located—Nicaragua, for instance.

Richard H. Ullman, *Minneapolis Tribune,* July 21, 1983.

Let's look at the interests offered by the administration to justify U.S. involvement in Central America.

First, U.S. *economic interests* in the region are currently marginal—less than 2 percent of U.S. investments abroad are in Central America and less than 2 percent of our trade is with the region. Moreover, the long-standing fear that the establishment of Communist regimes would close the "open door" of Western trade and investment has been questioned by none other than David Rockefeller, who in 1982 returned from a trip to Africa and declared that Americans could do business with the Communist regimes there if the U.S. government would let them.

While an impressive quantity of U.S. trade flows through the region, what country would seriously consider either trying to sink U.S. vessels or closing one of the strategic sea lanes? Certainly, the Cuban leadership understands that to do so would provide the U.S. government with the kind of pretext to punish Cuba militarily that many Americans have been seeking for the past twenty years.

As long as we support the principle of freedom of the seas, the Soviet navy will be able to conduct regular naval maneuvers in the Caribbean as it has done since 1969. One Cuba is more than adequate to service the needs of the Soviet fleet in the Caribbean. (A facility on the Pacific side of Central America, where there is less traffic, would be another matter.) Soviet interference with our shipping is unlikely short of a nuclear exchange, which would make any further discussion irrelevant. Even if there were a conventional war with the Soviets, it is unlikely that Cuba or other Soviet allies in the Caribbean would risk interfering with U.S. shipping, because of their extraordinary vulnerability to U.S. retaliation. Anyway, not much could be done that we aren't already doing to make the sea lanes less vulnerable. Undoubtedly, the Pentagon will insist on building up its capabilities in the Caribbean and will argue that an increased Cuban military buildup requires still larger budgets, though the threat is not directly against the U.S. but rather against other sovereign nations in the region, which have the option of turning to the OAS or the U.S. for defense if they feel the need.

That is not to suggest that we have no *security interests* in the region, only that traditional exhortations about strategic arteries or Soviet bases or expanded military capabilities in surrogate Cubas don't strike the same chord in Americans that they once did. This is because the administration's case against the Soviet threat to this hemisphere is a caricature, based on three exaggerated assertions.

Guerrillas As Soviet Tools

First, the administration argues that the guerrillas fighting in Central America are merely tools of the Soviet Union and Cuba. Reagan told the *Wall Street Journal* during the presidential campaign that the Soviet Union is the source of all instability in the Third World. . . .

This caricature of the guerrillas as tools only invites people to embrace a mirror-image caricature of the guerrillas as a wholly indigenous and autonomous response to decades of oppression and repression. The second caricature obscures the political, military, and ideological links between Central American revolutionaries and the Soviet Union and Cuba and the extent to which the guerrilla leaders look to Castro's Cuba as a political and military, if not an economic, model and at the U.S. as the source of all their nations' problems. (It is true that the left is quite heterogeneous, including disaffected Social and Christian Democrats in El Salvador, for example, but the guerrilla leaders with the guns do not hide their Marxism-Leninism in interviews with the Mexican and Cuban press, although they do sound more like Social Democrats when interviewed by American reporters.) Surely, a more realistic appraisal of the guerrilla movements in Central America would recognize their indigenous roots and their ideological branches, their idealistic motives and their hunger for power by force of arms, their professed interest in "democracy" and their own authoritarian organizations, their concern about social injustice and their belief in the class struggle, their admiration for Cuba and their obsessive hatred for "U.S. imperialism."

Second, the administration suggests that the emergence of "new Cubas" in Central America constitutes a security threat to the U.S. . . . The problem with this assertion is that the American people find it easier to visualize Central America as composed of six relatively poor and weak countries with a justifiable preference to be viewed in their own terms rather than as kings or pawns in a global chess game. . . .

Nicaragua's neighbors do have grounds for fearing that country's military buildup, but not because Nicaragua will invade, which would probably provoke an OAS response. When combined with Nicaragua's support for insurgencies in neighboring countries, the increased military capability acts to deter any neighbor from "hot pursuit." The U.S. is not the appropriate country and the State Department is not the appropriate forum, however, to make the case on Nicaragua's military buildup; the evidence should have been presented by Central American governments, with U.S. assistance, before the OAS, where a multilateral response could be requested.

The establishment of a Soviet base that could be used to threaten other countries or even the U.S. is a legitimate security concern, and a nation in the region that was on a collision course with the U.S. would certainly have an incentive to issue an invitation to the USSR, much as Cuba did in 1962. From a U.S. perspective, the issue is how to minimize the chance of this happening, and there are two ways: reduce the probability of Marxist-Leninists coming to power in the region who would look to the USSR and Cuba for security support, or try to reduce the level of hostility with such groups if they do come to power. Although some have referred to this concern with the possible emergence of hostile regimes as a presumption of U.S. hegemony or imperialism, in fact the concern is shared by all governments of the region, whether of the right, the left, or the center. However, this concern must be kept in perspective. The emergence of a hostile regime is primarily a regional problem affecting *important* U.S. interests, but it isn't one that alters the global strategic balance and threatens *vital* interests.

The administration's third assertion is that the choice for Central America is, in President Reagan's words, between "two different futures"—a positive, democratic one and a negative, Communist one. Would that it were so. Though the phrases are reminiscent of the Truman Doctrine of thirty-five years ago—and, unfortunately, of equal subtlety—the American people are not as trusting as they were then nor as ignorant of the real choices we face in Central America. As the U.S. retreats from its defense of human rights, the black-and-white choices begin to blur into one another. The Marxist future in Central America—at least as it has evolved in Nicaragua thus far—is simply not as dark as the administration would have us believe, and the possibility of a democratic future for El Salvador and Guatemala can hardly be considered bright.

Americans Unable to Choose

It is precisely because the likely alternatives are not very attractive that some Americans are driven to the idea that there is *no* choice. Others feel that the dissolution of the old oligarchical structure can present an opening for greater freedom and justice, and that it's a mistake to believe that if the left comes to power, it cannot be co-opted. Of course, U.S. policies can make revolutionaries either a little more or a little less hostile, but the probabilities argue against the chances of converting those Marxist-Leninist guerrillas, who have been fighting U.S. imperialism for a decade or so, into either democrats or friends of the U.S.

Underlying Motives

Two underlying motives explain the Reagan policy toward Central America.

The first is not "national security" but "national insecurity"—the psycho-political discomfort of accepting a loss of control, even when what is being controlled is no longer intrinsically very important, and when the costs of maintaining the control are very high and increasing. It is entirely understandable that national leaders find it hard to accept a loss of control of what used to be taken for granted. . . .

The second reason behind the deepening U.S. involvement in Central America is political. The President and his key advisers apparently believe that they would be vulnerable if El Salvador were to fall to the insurrectionists before the next U.S. election.

Abraham E. Lowenthal, *Los Angeles Times*, June 28, 1983.

In the search for a relevant answer to the old strategic question, we have ricocheted between two caricatures—one suggesting that our most vital security interests are at stake, and the other, that there are no objective security interests, only errant perceptions based on a lingering desire for hegemony. In assuming that the insurgencies are not nationalistic movements but rather tools of the Soviets and therefore fixed in their hostility to the U.S., that the cause of the instability is external, that the only struggle in Central America is against the left, the Reagan Administration distorts the struggle into a confrontation with the USSR and invests the prestige of the U.S. in the outcome, over which we have considerably less than complete control. Moreover, the strategy of bringing the full weight of the U.S. against the insurgents is counterproductive, because it provides the right with a blank check to be intransigent and repressive in its war against communism and the left with a target that it can use to establish its nationalist credentials. . . .

Those who would withdraw from Central America because they don't perceive any security interest either don't see or don't care about the covert extension of Cuban influence on behalf of Marxist-Leninist revolutionaries, or don't want to do anything about rightist terrorism, or don't think we can do anything. But they should understand that the consequence of withdrawal would be the intensification of the struggle; the right would be unshackled, and the Communist supporters of the left would be less inhibited in transferring weapons.

The question of national-security interests returns at one point or another to the question of U.S. *ideological interests*—human rights, democratic government, a pluralistic and open international system. . . . It is a mistake to view our security and human rights interests as contradictory; they are mutually reinforcing. Let me illustrate this point with two sets of examples. In the early 1970s, U.S. preoccupation with stability led us to ignore the discrediting of the democratic process in Nicaragua, El Salvador, and Guatemala, and the entire region is suffering because of the closing of those political avenues. In 1978, the U.S. placed its full weight behind democracy in Honduras and Panama, and that weight contributed to restraining the military in both countries, which are now relative paragons of stability.

Jeane Kirkpatrick, the U.S. ambassador to the United Nations, argues that the U.S. should have openly supported Somoza in Nicaragua, because the Sandinistas are worse. That same logic would lead us to resist all changes and to embrace all dictators—since the alternatives are almost always more uncertain. The Nicaraguan people had a lot more to say about whether Somoza remained in power than did the U.S., but even if the U.S. had had the choice, and backed Somoza, not only would we have backed a loser but we would have tainted our nation's values perhaps irrevocably in the area. Nothing would have weakened the U.S. security position more than to have gone down with Somoza. . . .

The migration is slowly changing the way the U.S. looks at itself and at Central America and the entire Caribbean Basin. . . .so will the new immigrants from Central America force our nation to watch that region with more sensitivity and concern.

The U.S. will continue to have a major impact on Central America, but the nature of that impact will change as Central America's presence begins to be felt more directly in the U.S. Some of the most important U.S. interests in the world derive from the interests and concerns of our multi-ethnic population. The "Caribbeanization" of the U.S. may very well be one of our most compelling and enduring interests in Central America.

U.S. strength is derived from its respect for political diversity abroad and at home. We have an interest in influencing developments in Central America but not in dominating those countries as the Soviet Union dominates Eastern Europe. The U.S. would not be served by a Reagan Corollary to the Brezhnev Doctrine.

"Our military support is essential."

Intervention Is Serving US Interests

Mortimer B. Zuckerman

Mortimer B. Zuckerman is president and chairman of The Atlantic Monthly Company, which publishes *The Atlantic* magazine. His degrees include a B.A. in economics and political theory from McGill University in Montreal, an M.B.A. from the University of Pennsylvania, and an L.L.B. from Harvard. In the following viewpoint, Mr. Zuckerman explains why, after a visit to Central America, he believes that US military support is necessary to protect our national and political interests in that region.

As you read, consider the following questions:

1. Why does the author believe the Sandinista government is a disappointment in Nicaragua?
2. What improvements in El Salvador has US intervention brought about, according to the author?
3. Does the author believe that military pressure has brought the Sandinistas closer to negotiating?

Because of enormous public confusion over the United States' involvement in Central America, I recently visited the region with a delegation of Congressmen to see it first-hand. I went holding political views of El Salvador and Nicaragua shared by many liberals and centrists in our nation. I returned impressed with the effectiveness of United States policy and convinced that we need to be involved.

I had thought that in El Salvador we were engaged in wrong-headed and dangerous military action on behalf of a repressive Government, and that Washington had failed to address economic and political grievances built up after decades of injustice. I went with the impression that the guerrillas seemed to have won popular support for their efforts to revolutionize the political system. My instinct was that this was only an internal struggle, not an East-West competition, and that once again we were backing the wrong side for the wrong reason.

But I returned home with the sense that United States military support was critical for physical security in the countryside, which, in turn, is necessary to guarantee ordinary Salvadoran's ability to make free choices. I also concluded that our military support is essential if we are to persuade the Salvadoran Government to democratize the political process and implement a program of agrarian reform and economic development. The guerrillas seem to have no larger a popular base than the Government does: Both sides command support with guns.

Nicaragua Is Totalitarian

In Nicaragua, the Sandinista revolution carried the hope for a better and freer life after the feudal tyranny of the United States-supported Somoza regime. Yet what I found was a Government busily consolidating a left-wing totalitarian state internally, and aggressively involved in attempting to overthrow its neighbors. It is the pressure of the United States-backed threat of a military confrontation that has produced the Sandinistas' first clear willingness to negotiate a genuine agreement not to destabilize their neighbors.

In El Salvador, the masses have not been angered to the point of large-scale popular uprisings like those in Nicaragua or Cuba. No popular revolt accompanied the guerrillas' "final" offensive in 1980-81, and last year's election showed that at least two-thirds of the people objected to being "liberated" by the revolutionary left. The guerrillas do not appear to have widespread popular support. In this situation, a military solution to control an insurgency is feasible.

To this end, the United States is training and equipping the Salvadoran Army for infantry and small-unit tactics and keeping the soldiers in the field to engage, harass and exhaust the guerrillas. We will have trained about 50 percent of the officers and noncommissioned officers by the end of 1983 in an effort to substitute effective combat leaders for those appointed for political loyalty. As a result, the Army has improved its morale and field performance and engaged in its most sustained and aggressive campaign. It has captured the momentum and substantial military control in much of the eastern provinces, particularly in San Vicente and Usulután. The rebels have withdrawn to remote areas, have not counter-attacked, have limited themselves to hit-and-run attacks and appear to have increasing logistical and manpower problems.

Intervention May Be Only Alternative

Morally, most Americans are reluctant to use any military force against small adversaries. Politically, a U.S. President's freedom to act decisively is hampered by an often reluctant Congress. And historically, Americans are still gun-shy from the frustrating failures in Korea and Vietnam.

The result is another dilemma: Americans do not want to let Communism gain a strategic base so close to home. But they are not yet willing to contemplate what may have to be done to prevent that, if economic and political strategies fail to deny further expansion to Soviet-Cuban power.

Thus, this giant nation could be rendered an almost helpless giant when it comes to opposing the Soviet style of expansionist aggression.

Marvin Stone, *U.S. News & World Report*, August 1, 1983.

In San Vicente, the Government has coordinated its military presence with programs in health, education, agriculture, transportation and reconstruction to retain the area's loyalty after the army leaves. This is a phase in an overall National Plan for Reconstruction. The cost of this program has been minimal by United States standards: only $65 million in military aid and $230 million in economic aid. Even the guerrilla political leader Ruben Zamora acknowledged to us that if this aid continues, the rebels can no longer hope to win the war.

The aid program also serves as leverage against the right-wing military. Only the United States can influence it to move away from a feudal political heritage of violence and vigilantism.

Military Impedes Reform

The left feeds off the rigidity of the right and military oppression and develops popular support by promising to redistribute

48

the wealth. It also benefits when rightist oligarchies buckle under economic pressures. The best way to diminish popular support for a violent Communist revolution is to open up the political channels and institute agrarian and economic reform. This can take place only when there is no widespread military insurgency.

Our pressure brought about last year's Salvadoran election and this year's negotiations for drafting a new constitution leading to presidential elections in 1984. Elections may be only "one note in the song of democracy," as a Salvadoran clergyman put it, but they represent legitimization of potential civilian control over military and paramilitary forces. Both have perpetrated atrocities that, if allowed to continue, will turn the masses implacably hostile. Our pressure is thus necessary on two counts: to prevent an extremist left-wing takeover while pushing the Government toward rights and democracy.

Fighting Against the Yanqui

However, no amount of change will end the Salvadoran conflict if Nicaragua, which regionalized the conflict in Central America, continues to fuel it. When they took over, the Sandinistas feared and hated the United States because of its patronage of Anastasio Somoza Debayle and military invasions over the past 130 years. The Sandinista hymn is "We fight against the Yanqui, enemy of humanity." President Jimmy Carter attempted to offset this by extending economic aid and friendship, but the Sandinistas remained convinced that the revolution would be safe from our intervention only if governments similar to their own were installed elsewhere in Central America. The Sandinistas set out to implement their slogan "revolution without boundaries."

In 1980, the Sandinistas, with Cuban advisers brought the five main guerrilla factions from El Salvador together in Managua, worked out a unity pact, set up joint command and control structures, organized training and logistical support on Nicaraguan soil and provided initial arms supplies. A Salvadoran rebel leader, Mario Aguinada, told us that support for training, logistics and command continues.

In Costa Rica, we were told that the Sandinistas are engaged there in a major propaganda campaign and are encouraging unrest, including infiltration in the northern provinces. The attempt to destabilize Costa Rica, a democracy without an army since 1948, is the clearest indication of Sandinista intentions.

Inside Nicaragua, the Sandinistas began and continued a program of totalitarian consolidation of power. The elements of the broader anti-Somoza coalition were discarded one by one—the Roman Catholic Church, other political parties, the press. The only Jewish community center and synagogue were seized and burned. The Sandinistas built the largest military force in Cental America. A Cuban-style pattern, with a widespread Cuban presence, has emerged.

To contain an interventionist Nicaragua, Washington sought—unsuccessfully—negotiations four times to bring about noninterference in neighboring territory and limits on Nicaragua's military buildup and the institutionalization of democratic opposition to create internal brakes on aggression. Rebuffed diplomatically, the United States moved militarily, ordering exercises, including fleet deployment. The Central Intelligence Agency expanded its support of the "contras"—the anti-Government guerrillas that harass the countryside. We continue to train and equip the Honduran Army, which Nicaragua considers its most dangerous regional miltary adversary. A border shootout in May with Nicaragua brought about full mobilization of the Honduran Army, signaling its participation in any military crisis in the region.

Military Pressure Aids Change

The cumulative military pressure organized by the Reagan Administration has resulted in a major shift in Sandinista policy. In our meetings with the Sandinista leadership, we were told that Nicaragua was prepared to negotiate verifiable nonintervention in neighboring territories, especially El Salvador. This change appeared to be due exclusively to the perception that the United States had been provoked to the point that a military confrontation was possible.

The United States has long supported repressive rightist regimes, sometimes by using our troops. We must develop an alternative to such regimes—and those of the left—by opening up Latin American political and economic processes. Our interests are involved because what happens in Nicaragua and El Salvador can affect Mexico or the Panama Canal. Central America is on our strategic doorstep. We cannot remain above the fray.

"Many of our countries are struggling to cease being banana republics. . . .Do not force them to choose between appealing to the Soviet Union or capitulating to the United States."

Intervention Is Not Serving US Interests

Carlos Fuentes

Carlos Fuentes is a Mexican writer, editor, and diplomat. He is the former Mexican Ambassador to France and was head of the department of cultural relations in the Mexican Ministry of Foreign Affairs. He is famous for his fiction, much of which is a synthesis of reality and fantasy. His novels include *Terra Nostra*, *The Death of Artemio Cruz*, and *Aqua Quemada*. In the following viewpoint, Mr. Fuentes declares that formulated US interests, such as democracy and stability in Central America, are actually being undermined by the United States' continual "big stick" attitude.

As you read, consider the following questions:

1. How does the Mexican Revolution exemplify other Central American revolutions, according to Mr. Fuentes?
2. Does the author believe Central American struggles are internally or externally motivated? What reasons does he give?
3. How, in Mr. Fuentes' opinion, can America set an example for Central America?

"High Noon in Latin America," by Carlos Fuentes. Published in Vanity Fair. Copyright © 1983 by Carlos Fuentes. Reprinted by permission of Brandt & Brandt Literary Agents Inc.

Some time ago, I was traveling in the state of Morelos in central Mexico, looking for the birthplace of Emiliano Zapata, the village of Anenecuilco. I stopped on the way and asked a *campesino*, a laborer of the fields, how far it was to that village. He answered me: "If you had left at daybreak, you would be there now." This man had an internal clock which marked his own time and that of his culture. For the clocks of all men and women, of all civilizations, are not set at the same hour. One of the wonders of our menaced globe is the variety of its experiences, its memories and its desires. Any attempt to impose a uniform politics on this diversity is like a prelude to death.

The daybreak of a movement of social and political renewal cannot be set by calendars other than those of the people involved. Revolutions cannot be exported. With Lech Walesa and Solidarity, it was the internal clock of the people of Poland that struck the morning hour. So it has always been: with the people of Massachusetts in 1776; with the people of my country during our revolutionary experience; with the people of Central America in the hour we are all living. The dawn of revolution reveals the total history of a community. This is a self-knowledge that a society cannot be deprived of without grave consequences.

The Mexican Revolution was the object of constant harassment, pressures, menaces, boycotts, and even a couple of armed interventions between 1910 and 1932. It was extremely difficult for the United States administrations of the time to deal with violent and rapid change on the southern border of your country. Calvin Coolidge convened both houses of Congress in 1927 and—talkative for once—denounced Mexico as the source of "Bolshevik" subversion in Central America. This set the scene for the third invasion of Nicaragua by U.S. Marines in this century. We were the first domino. But precisely because of our revolutionary policies (favoring agrarian reform, secular education, collective bargaining, and recovery of natural resources)—all of them opposed by the successive governments in Washington, from Taft to Hoover—Mexico became a modern, contradictory, self-knowing and self-questioning nation.

Mexican Revolution and Democracy

The revolution did not make an instant democracy out of my country. Mexico first had to become a nation. What the revolution gave us all was the totality of our history and the possibility of a culture. "The revolution," wrote my compatriot, the great poet Octavio Paz, "is a sudden immersion of Mexico in its own being. In the revolutionary explosion. . .each Mexican. . .finally recognizes, in a mortal embrace, the other Mexican." How can we stand by as this experience is denied, through ignorance and arrogance, to other people, our brothers, in Central America and the Caribbean?

The United States is the only major power of the West that was born beyond the Middle Ages, modern at birth. As part of the fortress of the Counter-Reformation, Latin America has had to do constant battle with the past. We did not acquire freedom of speech, freedom of belief, freedom of enterprise as our birthrights, as you did. We have had to fight desperately for them. The complexity of the cultural struggles underlying our political and economic struggles has to do with unresolved tensions, sometimes as old as the conflict between pantheism and monotheism, or as recent as the conflict between tradition and modernity. This is our cultural baggage, both heavy and rich.

The problems of Nicaragua are Nicaraguan, but they will cease to be so if that country is deprived of all possibility for normal survival. Why is the United States so impatient with four years of Sandinismo, when it was so tolerant of forty-five years of Somocismo? Why is it so worried about free elections in Nicaragua, but so indifferent to free elections in Chile? And why, if it respects democracy so much, did the United States not rush to the defense of the democratically elected president of Chile, Salvador Allende, when he was overthrown by the Latin American Jaruzelski, General Augusto Pinochet? How can we live and grow together on the basis of such hypocrisy?

Nicaragua is being attacked and invaded by forces sponsored

1984, The Philadelphia Inquirer, Washington Post Writers Group, reprinted with permission.

by the United States. It is being invaded by counter-revolutionary bands led by former commanders of Somoza's national guard who are out to overthrow the revolutionary government and reinstate the old tyranny. Who will stop them from doing so if they win? These are not freedom fighters. They are Benedict Arnolds.

The problems of El Salvador, are Salvadoran. The Salvadoran rebellion did not originate and is not manipulated from outside El Salvador. To believe this is akin to crediting Soviet accusations that the Solidarity movement in Poland is somehow the creature of the United States.

Real Struggle an Internal One

The real struggle for Latin America is then, as always, a struggle with ourselves, within ourselves. We must solve it by ourselves. Nobody else can truly know it; we are living through our family quarrels. We must assimilate this conflicted past. Sometimes we must do it—as has occurred in Mexico, Cuba, El Salvador and Nicaragua—through violent means. We need time and culture. We also need patience. Both ours and yours.

What happens between the daybreak of revolution in a marginal country and its imagined destiny as a Soviet base? If nothing happens but harassment, blockades, propaganda, pressures, and invasions against the revolutionary country, then that prophecy will become self-fulfilling.

But if power with historical memory and diplomacy with historical imagination come into play, we, the United States and Latin America, might end up with something very different: a Latin America of independent states building institutions of stability, renewing the culture of national identity, diversifying our economic interdependence, and wearing down the dogmas of two musty nineteenth-century philosophies. And a United States giving the example of a tone in relations that is present, active, co-operative, respectful, aware of cultural differences, and truly proper for a great power unafraid of ideological labels, capable of coexisting with diversity in Latin America as it has learned to coexist with diversity in black Africa.

Precisely twenty years ago, John F. Kennedy said at another commencement ceremony: "If we cannot end now our differences, at least we can help make the world safe for diversity." This, I think, is the greatest legacy of the sacrificed statesman whose death we all mourned. Let us understand that legacy, by which death ceased to be an enigma and became, not a lament for what might have been, but a hope for what can be. This can be.

Let us remember, let us imagine, let us reflect. The United States can no longer go it alone in Central America and the Caribbean. It cannot, in today's world, practice the anachronistic policies of the "big stick." It will only achieve, if it does so, what it cannot truly want. Many of our countries are struggling to cease being banana republics. They do not want to become balalaika republics. Do not force them to choose between appealing to the Soviet Union or capitulating to the United States.

My plea is this one: Do not practice negative overlordship in this hemisphere. Practice positive leadership. Join the forces of change and patience and identity in Latin America.

Intervention Won't Prevent Revolution

I do not believe that revolution is an exportable item. I am not hiding that revolutionary Cuba has offered its active solidarity to other Latin American revolutionaries in countries where, as in the case of Somoza's Nicaragua, all democratic action and all possibility of protest other than armed struggle was ruled out by brutal terror. Nor am I hiding the fact that when a large group of Latin American countries, under the inspiration and guidance of Washington, not only tried to isolate Cuba politically, but economically blockaded it and helped sponsor sabotage, armed infiltrations, assassination attempts, we responded by helping all those who wanted to fight such governments.

We were not the ones to start subversion, it was they. Actually, we can neither export revolution nor can the United States prevent it. Reagan is cunningly using this argument to frighten the U.S. people, by fanning a primitive anticommunism. These arguments enable Reagan to conduct a policy of overt intervention such as the one brutally carried out against Grenada, a tiny island with a population of 100,000 people.

Newsweek, Interview with Fidel Castro, January 9, 1984.

"If we had started out at daybreak, we would be there now." Our times have not coincided. Your daybreak came quickly. Our night has been long. But we can overcome the distance between our times if we can both recognize that the true duration of the human heart is in the present, this present in which we remember and we desire; this present where our past and our future are gone.

We need your memory and your imagination or ours shall never be complete. You need our memory to redeem your past, and our imagination to complete your future. We may be here on this hemisphere for a long time. Let us remember one another. Let us respect one another. Let us walk together outside the night of repression and hunger and intervention, even if for you the sun is at high noon and for us at a quarter to twelve.

Ranking American Foreign Policy Concerns

This activity will give you an opportunity to discuss with classmates the values you and your classmates consider important in foreign policy and the values you believe are considered most important by the majority of Americans.

Michael Keefe for the Denver Post, reprinted with permission.

This cartoon examines US foreign policy concerns. The authors of this chapter all debate US foreign policy priorities within the context of US involvement in Central America. Many believe American political values are becoming twisted, and that the US has no right to intervene in other countries' affairs. Others, however, believe our involvement is essential.

Part 1

Step 1.   The class should break into groups of four to six students and discuss the meaning of the Keefe cartoon.

Step 2.   Working individually within each group, each student should rank the foreign policy concerns listed below, assigning the number 1 to the concern he or she personally considers most important, the number 2 to the second most important concern, and so on, until all values have been ranked.

Step 3.   Students should compare their rankings with others in the group, giving the reasons for their rankings.

_____ protecting national security
_____ protecting human rights
_____ promoting democracy in other countries
_____ defeating communism
_____ promoting self-reliance in other countries
_____ promoting friendship between countries
_____ promoting free elections
_____ ending dictatorships
_____ supporting governments friendly to the US
_____ providing economic aid to poor countries
_____ providing military aid to stem revolutions

Part 2

Step 1.   Working in groups of four to six students, each group should rank the concerns listed in what the group considers the order of importance to the majority of Americans. Assign the number 1 to the concern the group believes is most important to the majority of Americans, and so on until all the concerns have been ranked.

Step 2.   Each group should compare its ranking with others in a classwide discussion.

Step 3.   The entire class should discuss the following questions.

1. What noticeable differences do you see between personal rankings in Part 1 and the perceived ranking of the majority of Americans in Part 2?

2. How would you explain these differences?

3. What conclusions would you draw about the direction America's future foreign policy would take if you examine: (a) the majority of Americans' foreign policy rankings of Part 2, (b) your own rankings of concerns in Part 1, and (c) the ranking the cartoon indicates the US follows now?

Periodical Bibliography

The following list of periodical articles deals with the subject matter of this chapter.

Robert A. Dahl	"The Democratic Mystique," *The New Republic*, April 2, 1984.
Eva Gold	"Time Bomb with a Lit Fuse," *The Christian Century*, April 25, 1984.
Harper's	"Why Are We In Central America? On Dominoes, Death Squads and Democracy," June 1984.
Roland S. Homet Jr.	"Foreign Policy Lessons from the Central America Diversion," *USA Today*, July 1983.
Jeane Kirkpatrick	"U.S. Security and Latin America," *Commentary*, January 1981.
Langhorne A. Motley	"El Salvador: Revolution or Reform?" *Department of State Bulletin*, March 1984.
The Nation	January 28, 1984, special issue on Central America.
The New Republic	"The Central America Wars," May 23, 1983.
Ronald Reagan	"Saving Freedom in Central America," *Department of State Bulletin*, April 1983.
Ronald Reagan	News conference, *Department of State Bulletin*, September 1983.
William D. Rogers	"The Stakes in El Salvador," *Newsweek* March 30, 1981.
George Shultz	"Strengthening Democracy in Central America," *Department of State Bulletin* April 1983.
Jeff Stein	Interview with Robert E. White, "The Day of Reckoning Is Coming," *The Progressive*, September 1981.
James W. Wall	"What if 'They' Sink Another Maine?" *The Christian Century*, July 20/27, 1983.
Margaret P. Wilde	"What Good Would It Do to Stop the War?" *The Christian Century*, May 2, 1984.

Is US Involvement in Central America Justified?

*"We can and must help Central America....
Morally, it's the only right thing to do."*

US Involvement in Central America Is Morally Right

Ronald Reagan

Ronald Reagan was elected to a second term as president of the United States in 1984. His policy continued to be one of lending aid to and supporting intervention in Central America. In the following viewpoint, President Reagan sanctions US military appropriations to Central America as being the United States' moral duty.

As you read, consider the following questions:

1. What, according to President Reagan, was the United States' policy toward the Somoza regime?
2. How is US support in El Salvador protecting human rights there, according to Reagan?
3. Why, according to Ronald Reagan, must we stop Communism from spreading?

Ronald Reagan in a speech delivered on national television from the White House on May 9, 1984.

The defense policy of the United States is based on a simple premise: We do not start wars. We will never be the aggressor. We maintain our strength in order to deter and defend against aggression—to preserve freedom and peace. We help our friends defend themselves.

Central America is a region of great importance to the United States. And it is so close—San Salvador is closer to Houston than Houston is to Washington, D.C. Central America is America; it is at our doorstep. And it has become the stage for a bold attempt by the Soviet Union, Cuba and Nicaragua to install Communism by force throughout the hemisphere....

Communist Aggression

We can and must help Central America. It's in our national interest to do so, and morally, it's the only right thing to do. But helping means doing enough—enough to protect our security and enough to protect the lives of our neighbors so that they may live in peace and democracy without the threat of Communist aggression and subversion. This has been the policy of our Administration for more than three years.

But making this choice requires a commitment from all of us, our Administration, the American people and the Congress. So far, we have not yet made that commitment. We have provided just enough aid to avoid outright disaster but not enough to resolve the crisis, so El Salvador is being left to slowly bleed to death....

The people of Central America want democracy and freedom. They want and hope for a better future. Costa Rica is a well-established and healthy democracy. Honduras made a peaceful transition to democracy in 1982. And in Guatemala, political parties and trade unions are functioning. An election is scheduled for July there, with a real prospect that that country can return to full constitutional government in 1985.

In fact, 26 of 33 Latin American countries are democracies or striving to become democracies. But they are vulnerable.

By aiding the Communist guerrillas in El Salvador, Nicaragua's unelected Government is trying to overthrow the duly-elected Government of a neighboring country. Like Nicaragua, the Government of El Salvador was born of revolution, but unlike Nicaragua it has held three elections, the most recent a presidential election last Sunday. It has made great progress toward democracy. In this last election, 80 percent of the people in El Salvador braved Communist threats and guerrilla violence to vote for peace and freedom.

Let me give another example of the difference between the two countries—El Salvador and Nicaragua. The Government of El Salvador has offered amnesty to the guerrillas and asked them to participate in the elections and democratic progress. The guerrillas refused; they want to shoot their way into power and establish totalitarian rule.

By contrast, the contras, the freedom-fighters in Nicaragua, have offered to lay down their weapons and take part in democratic elections; but there the communist Sandinista Government has refused.

That's why the United States must support both the elected Government of El Salvador and the democratic aspirations of the Nicaraguan people.

If the Communists can start war against the people of El Salvador, then El Salvador and its friends are surely justified in defending themselves by blocking the flow of arms. If the Soviet Union can aid and abet subversion in our hemisphere, then the United States has a legal right and a moral duty to help resist it. This is not only in our strategic interest; it is morally right. It would be profoundly immoral to let peace-loving friends depending on our help be overwhelmed by brute force if we have any capacity to prevent it.

Contras Are Democratic

The democratic commitment of the Contras seems clear. Of its seven-man directorate, only one member, Enrique Bermudez, was a follower of Somoza—and even he was exiled by Somoza in the final days of his regime. Most of the leaders are members of the former Conservative Party, established by the assassination anti-Somoza editor, Pedro Joaquin Chamorro.

While in Honduras this writer has also had a chance to visit a refugee camp on the Nicaraguan border, where thousands of Nicaraguans have fled from the Sandinista regime. Life in such camps is bleak, in one instance 27 members of a family lived in a single room. Why did they leave? One man, a peasant, said: "The Sandinistas took our crop from us, leaving us not enough to eat. They raped our women. They began to educate our children in atheism. They took the young men to serve their army." Was life preferable under the previous regime? "Under Somoza," he replied, echoing the views we repeatedly heard, "we were left alone. It was much better."

Allan C. Brownfeld, *Washington Inquirer*, July 10, 1983.

If our political process pulls together, Soviet- and Cuban-supported aggression can be defeated. On this, the centennial and anniversary of President Harry Truman's birth, it is fitting to recall his words, spoken to a Joint Session of the Congress in a similar situation: "The free peoples of the world look to us for support in maintaining their freedoms. If we falter...we may endanger the peace of the world, and we shall surely endanger the welfare of this nation."

The speech was given in 1947. The problem then was two years of Soviet-supported indirect aggression against Greece. The Communists were close to victory. President Truman called on the Congress to provide decisive aid to the Greek government. Both parties rallied behind President Truman's call. Democratic forces succeeded and Greece became a parliamentary democracy....

Let's remember, the Soviet bloc gave Cuba and Nicaragua $4.9 billion in assistance last year, while the United States provided all its friends throughout Central America with only a fraction of that amount.

Will We Support Freedom?

The simple questions are: Will we support freedom in this hemisphere or not? Will we defend our vital interests in this hemisphere or not? Will we stop the spread of Communism in this hemisphere or not? Will we act while there is still time?

There are those in this country who would yield to the temptation to do nothing. They are the new isolationists, very much like the isolationists of the late 1930's who knew what was happening in Europe but chose not to face the terrible challenge history had given them. They preferred a policy of wishful thinking that if they only gave up one more country, allowed just one more international transgression, then surely, sooner or later, the aggressor's appetite would be satisfied....

As I talk to you tonight, there are young Salvadoran soliders in the field facing the terrorists and guerrillas in El Salvador with the clips in their rifles the only ammunition they have. The lack of evacuation helicopters for the wounded and the lack of medical supplies if they are evacuated has resulted in one out of three of the wounded dying. This is no way to support friends—particularly when supporting them is supporting ourselves....

It's up to all of us, the Administration, you as citizens, and your representatives in the Congress. The people of Central America can succeed if we provide the assistance I have proposed. We Americans should be proud of what we are trying to do in Central America and proud of what, together with our friends, we can do in Central America—to support democracy, human rights and economic growth while preserving peace so close to home. Let us show the world that we want no hostile, Communist colonies here in the Americas: South, Central or North.

"We must recognize that the United States itself is responsible for destroying the political process in El Salvador, as well as the backbone of its economy."

US Involvement in Central America Is Morally Wrong

Jesse Helms

Jesse Helms is a Republican US senator from North Carolina. He is chairman of the Committee on Foreign Relations, assistant minority whip, and serves on several senate committees such as the Select Committee on Ethics, the Rules Committee, and the Committee on Agriculture, Nutrition and Forestry. His honors include the Conservative Congressional Award and the Southern Baptist National Award for Service to Mankind. In the following viewpoint, Senator Helms concludes that US involvement in El Salvador is morally wrong and argues that all previous US involvement served only to increase problems in the region.

As you read, consider the following questions:

1. What does Senator Helms think of the US sponsored military coup in El Salvador?
2. Are US policies ultimately supporting democracy in El Salvador, according to Mr. Helms?

Jesse Helms, in hearings before the Committee on Foreign Relations of the United States Senate, March 22, 23, and 24, 1983.

I think it is time that we all took a step backwards and take a look at what we are doing in this action—what we are doing not only to ourselves but to this country.

Here we are trying to second-guess not only every action of our own administration, but also the actions of the elected Government of El Salvador.

I think we all recognize that the situation in El Salvador is far from normal or desirable. We have a country that has been destabilized from one side by international Marxism and socialism, and destabilized from the other side by the United States.

We must recognize that the United States itself is responsible for destroying the politice l process in El Salvador, as well as the backbone of its economy.

I well remember sitting in this committee room and the committee room over in the Dirksen Building and listening to some members of this committee—some of whom are no longer members of this committee. They sat here and gave orders to a U.S. Ambassador to go to El Salvador and be the U.S. Pro-Consul—that is the word that was used, the exact word, with all of the overtones of Yankee imperialism that are supposedly anathema to all liberal-minded citizens of the republic. Yet, "Pro-Consul" was the word and Pro-Consul that Ambassador set out to be.

I would also remind the committee, with all due respect and affection, that the United States Government had already organized a military coup that set aside the constitutional Government of El Salvador. That was not such a terrific government, we all know that, but at least it was constitutional and it had been elected.

After that, the United States installed its own hand-picked president, without benefit of further elections. When the U.S. Ambassador went down there he proceeded to work exclusively with what he called, the democratic left. Those are not my words, those are his words.

Furthermore, his duties as Pro-Consul included magic solutions such as so-called land reform, nationalization of the banks, and nationalization of the export system.

Now, the point is this, Mr. Chairman, even if these had been good ideas—and they were terrible ideas—it was like ordering a heart transplant when the patient had tuberculosis. Those programs were blatantly illegal and unconstitutional under the Salvadoran constitution, and we hardly even asked whether these were good ideas or whether they would work.

What did these ideas do? They disrupted not only the economic system but the political system as well. They instilled fear, uncertainty, greed, and hatred. There could have been

YOUR TAX | DOLLARS AT

WORK IN | EL SALVADOR.

Clay Bennet, *St. Petersburg Times*, reprinted with permission.

nothing better calculated to polarize the nation and make it impossible to heal the wounds and work toward a better standard of living for everyone. These programs did nothing to improve living conditions, instead they made matters worse.

The Marxists, supported by the Soviet-Cuban alliance aimed their blows at the very fabric of the nation, trying to make it impossible for the ordinary citizen to earn a living or to carry on a normal life.

There is no doubt that everything the United States did made matters worse, not better.

Now, our intentions were undoubtedly good, I do not question that. But it is manifestly impossible to dictate the reform of a society from the outside. That is what we have been trying to do. That is what we are trying to do here today, right here in this committee.

Now, despite these obviously wrongheaded and heavyhanded efforts, the Salvadorans went to the polls 1 year ago in a massive and courageous turnout. Under the worst possible conditions the Salvadorans embraced democracy. The result of that election was to turn out the unelected president that had been installed by whom? By the United States.

Did we learn a lesson? No, we did not. We promptly put on tremendous pressure to install yet another president who did not reflect the mandate of the voters. We also installed a military commander who was more keenly attuned to some voices in the U.S. Congress than to the military necessities of his nation.

So, here we are today making more mischief—and that is all it is, Mr. Chairman. We are trying to push the elected Government of El Salvador farther to the left, and no other face can be put on it. Some are even trying to force the freely elected government to share power with the totalitarian forces represented by the Marxist guerrillas.

If you want an analogy, what would have been the reaction years ago if it had been proposed that we bring in Al Capone for some negotiations, for participation in how to run the city of Chicago?

I think we have to ask ourselves what we want the result of this process to be. Do we really want a socialistic or a Marxist government in El Salvador? Do we think a socialist government is more just as a form of social organization than a free government? Is there any socialist government in the world where the people are better off than in a free government? If we can find one, let us pinpoint it.

Free Governments No Good?

If we would rather have a socialist government or a Marxist government in El Salvador, let us say so and not beat around the bush. Why do we not come out and tell the American people what we think about the situation? If we think that free governments are no good, let us say that.

Now, let us look at the specific process we are involved in here this morning. For the first time we are setting the precedent that the Foreign Relations Committee has the right to reject reprograming. We have not covered ourselves with glory in this attempt.

First of all, we do not have any authority under the law to do what we are doing. We are just trying to bully ourselves into the process. The administration has the authority to reprogram and we have no authority to stop it. Our only claim is the flame of blackmail. We are saying to the administration that if it does not follow our dictates and do what we want done, we are going to retaliate in some indefinite way.

I do not think that is the way to build a relationship of trust and cooperation with any administration.

The only shred of authority is the letter that we have from our former colleague in the Senate, Mr. Buckley, who was at that time Under Secretary of State. When we look at the Buckley letter—which was undoubtedly prepared by the Legal Adviser's

Office at the State Department—we see that we have practically nothing.

The letter assures us that the administration "will give full consideration and great weight to the views of the committee." Note those words, "full consideration and great weight." I dare say that many letters which many Senators have written to their constituents have contained the same phraseology, using a few words to say nothing. It is a polite formula which appears to promise more than is actually given. There is no promise to admit us to the decisionmaking process, only the promise that our objection will get full consideration.

I would like to think that our views would get full consideration whether we had the letter from Mr. Buckley or not.

The letter goes on to say, "We will make every effort to resolve differences before proceeding." That is a gracious statement. That is about all we could expect. But it is no more than we had a right to expect before that letter. So, we do not have much in this "thin reed" of a letter.

US Mischief Increasing

The mischief that we are trying to do on the basis of such a thin reed is very great. I think that most of us heard the President of the United States. He laid out for the American people what the situation is vis-à-vis the Soviet Union and the Caribbean.

I do think we ought to pretend that we can view El Salvador in isolation. If we do that, then we are encouraging the tumbling of all of Central America.

So, Mr. Chairman, with all due respect to my colleagues, I would say almost that we are about to make fools of ourselves. We talk of consensus and there is no consensus, that is obvious. The only consensus is that this committee does not seem willing to allow the Salvadoran people to decide their own future. The only consensus seems to be that we want to push them step by step into the hands of the Communists.

I think it is time that we put away our little legislative toys, adjourned this meeting, and went home.

"Nicaragua forces legitimate dissent at home to follow violent means and persists in threatening and destabilizing its neighbors."

US Opposition to Nicaragua Is Justified

Thomas O. Enders

Thomas O. Enders, former assistant secretary for Inter-American Affairs (1981-1983), is the US Ambassador to Spain. He earned a B.A. at Yale, an M.A. at Harvard, and a Docteur de l'Université from the University of Paris in France. He joined the US foreign service in 1958 and served as a government official in Stockholm and Vietnam. He was ambassador to Canada (1976-79) and ambassador to the European Communities (1979-81). In the following viewpoint, Mr. Enders states his belief that the US is supporting legitimate opposition forces which are seeking democracy in Nicaragua.

As you read, consider the following questions:

1. What are the three objectives the US is trying to convince Nicaragua to implement, according to Mr. Enders?
2. Who does the author believe are the two major opposition groups to the Sandinistas?
3. According to the author, to what group did the leaders of these groups originally belong?

Thomas O. Enders, in a statement before the House Foreign Affairs Committee on April 14, 1983.

Since the Somoza government collapsed and the Sandinistas came to power, U.S. policy toward Nicaragua has focused on attempting to convince Nicaragua to:

• Renounce support for insurgency in neighboring countries;

• Abandon its pursuit of dominant military power in Central America; and

• Come to terms with its own society through the creation of democratic institutions. . . .

We are not going to give up. The Sandinistas are obviously not yet persuaded that they have to negotiate on substance with either their neighbors or their internal critics. Perhaps they still think that if they bob and weave enough, something will change—that the United States will end or weaken its support for democratic governments in Costa Rica, El Salvador, and Honduras—and that the way will again be open for the "revolution without frontiers." We must convince them that is not the case, that the United States will not abandon its friends in Central America. At the same time, we must go on probing, proposing ways to think that overcome the old objections—until the Sandinistas tell us they are ready to move to a fair and equitable dialogue.

The Anti-Sandinista Insurgency

Meanwhile, Nicaraguans have taken matters into their own hands. The Sandinistas have begun to reap the consequences of their abandonment of the original goals of the Nicaraguan revolution. Sandinista intransigence has sparked an insurgency that the Sandinistas themselves claim is a threat. Several thousand guerrillas are now active in Nicaragua. Disillusioned Miskito Indians operate in much of their homeland in the Atlantic lowlands. In the eastern and northern border departments of Jinotega, Nueva Segovia, Madriz, Esteli, and Zelaya, significant insurgent forces are attacking government outposts and ambushing military convoys. Guerrilla activity is reported in the central coffee-growing province of Matagalpa. This month, for the first time, armed dissidence has been reported in the south. Wherever the opposition groups show up, they seem to attract local support, and their numbers grow.

In light of recent allegations in the media, you will ask me right off whether this insurgency has been created or supported by the United States. No American administration has ever discussed this kind of allegation—other than in the Senate and House committees created expressly for the purpose—and this one will not break precedent. But I will describe the Nicaraguan opposition movements; it should be clear to you that it has appeared and expanded in response to deep grievances against the Sandinistas.

Who are the people challenging Managua's ideologues? What do they want? From what we know, there are two major groups. Both are Nicaraguan to the core.

Frente Democrático Nacional. One, the larger, is the Frente Democratico Nacional (FDN). . . .

FDN pronouncements repudiate the Somoza past and affirm the nationalistic and patriotic principles of Sandino. As I am sure the committee is aware, the FDN proposed a peace plan on January 13, 1983, in which they offered to cease hostilities if, among other points, the Government of Nicaragua held internationally supervised elections by September 1983, revoked the state of siege in Nicaragua, and separated public administration from partisan political and ideological activities.

Aliánza Revolucionária Democrática. The second major group, led by the anti-Somoza hero Eden Pastora, is ARDE—the Aliánza Revolucionária Democrática.

Sandinistas and Broken Promises

The current Sandinist leadership has broken its promise to the Nicaraguan people. . . .

Sadly, the revolution's bright promise has not been realized. Instead, the Sandinist directorate has replaced the Somozas with a totalitarian tyranny whose sole aim has been to monopolize power. In pursuit of this goal, the directorate has consolidated its hegemony within the Sandinista party while harassing and rendering ineffectual other political groups. Directorate members speak about pluralism and possible elections in 1985—six years after Somoza's ouster! They are quick to add, however, that they have no intention of giving up power—or even a share of it—through the electoral process.

Eden Pastora, *The New York Times*, July 15, 1982.

ARDE's leaders include such well-known figures as former post-Somoza junta leader Alfonso Robelo, Miskito Indian leader Brooklyn Rivera, and former anti-Somoza fighter Fernando "Negro" Chamorro. Pastora, who was the original Sandinista Vice Minister of Defense, has repeatedly denounced the revolution's betrayal, which he argues was motivated by Cuban agents enforcing a sellout to the Soviet Union. "There can be no peace in Nicaragua," Pastora argues, "as long as the slaughter of the Miskitos, Sumus, and Ramas continues, as long as there is no freedom of the press, and as long as the occupation by Cuban, German, Soviet and Bulgárian troops continues."

Caught off balance by the scope of the opposition it has brought upon itself, the Nicaraguan Government has sought to discredit its opponents as "Somocistas"—attempting to associate them with the crimes of the former government. The Sandinistas' current propaganda plan—we have seen the March 24 FSLN [Sandinista National Liberation Front] memorandum—instructs its political cadres to blame "U.S. imperialism" for the country's problems, to smear Adolfo Calero, a Democratic Conservative Party leader with whom they have negotiated, and Alfonso Robelo, a former member of their own junta, as "traitors" and to portray opposition as aimed against Nicaragua rather than against its current rulers.

The Sandinista tactic is to assert that the only alternative to what they've created is "Somocismo." Nothing could be more simplistic or more false. "Somocismo" was a highly personal traditional dictatorship that died with Somoza. It could not be recreated even if one wished to do so. The Sandinistas know that most Nicaraguans want democracy, peace, and an end to Cuban influence. Indeed, that is the program promised the Nicaraguan people in 1979. And that is the program the Sandinistas are today always trying to sweep under the rug they call "Somocismo." The Nicaraguan people remember their history. So should we.

The Regional Question

It is not clear what the course of the struggle in Nicaragua will be. What is certain is that, as long as Nicaragua forces legitimate dissent at home to follow violent means and persists in threatening and destabilizing its neighbors, it will never be stable, nor will Central America.

It is conceivable that Cuba or the Soviet Union could be tempted to escalate the conflict, introducing modern fighter aircraft or even Cuban combat troops. Clearly, a dangerous situation would then develop, unacceptable not only to Central America but to the American nations as a whole. We have communicated to Moscow and Havana how dangerous such a move would be. It is also conceivable that, in an effort to distract attention from their internal problems, the Sandinistas might lash out at their neighbors, attacking Costa Rica or Honduras. For over a year, Managua has already been running terrorist operations in San José and infiltrating guerrillas into northern Costa Rican provinces. And there have been frequent border incidents with Honduras. Although journalists who have visited the area report no activity on the Honduran side, Nicaragua has recently reinforced military units on the border. Again, I believe the Sandinistas understand that they could not gain by attacking their neighbors. It is also important to stress that every resource of inter-American diplomacy, including, of course, that of this country, would be available to prevent such an outburst.

But there is a better way. It is through dialogue and negotiation. We ask the Sandinistas to think of the Nicaraguan people. Despite all that foreign aid, Nicaraguans in cities and countryside are much less well off than before the revolution. They resent the pressures on their churches and their clergy. They distrust and dislike the Sandinista monopoly of power—they have lived under such a system before.

We ask the Sandinistas to consider the insurgency in their own country. Despite (or is it because?) the presence of all those armed Cubans, popular resistance is spreading. They may conclude that the dialogue they have so many times spurned is preferable to widening civil strife.

We ask the Sandinistas to consider the insurgency they are supporting in El Salvador. If it has legitimate grievances, let them be pursued through democratic institutions. The international community is willing and able to provide security and other guarantees for elections as the answer there as well.

Each element of the Central American problem is related to the other. No amount of land reform, or open elections, or improvement in human rights will end the conflict in El Salvador if Nicaragua continues to fuel it. Democracy will not prosper in Nicaragua's neighbors unless it is practiced in Nicaragua as well. Nicaragua will not be free of the hostility of its own people and of its neighbors, until it begins to address their concerns for democracy and security.

So the answer is democratization and dialogue among neighbors. The purpose of U.S. policy in the area is to create conditions in which the area can be removed from East-West conflict, the import of offensive weapons and mutual support for insurgencies ended, and the democratic transformation of each society achieved. Negotiations among all the Central American countries and negotiations within countries can provide the opportunity for all groups to compete in the voting booth rather than on the battlefield.

"A U.S.-supported terrorist insurgency. . .has killed hundreds of civilians, devastated whole communities and increased misery and deprivation by crippling the country's economy."

US Opposition to Nicaragua Is Unjustified

Richard J. Barnet and Peter R. Kornbluh

Richard J. Barnet is a co-founder and a senior fellow of the Institute for Policy Studies (IPS) in Washington, D.C. An advisor in the State Department during the Kennedy administration, he is also the author of numerous books including *Real Security* and *The Alliance.* Peter R. Kornbluh is a research associate at IPS. He has an M.A. in international relations and is a specialist on US foreign policy in Latin America. In the following viewpoint, the authors contend that the US is attempting to overthrow the legitimate Sandinista government by supporting the *contra* movement.

As you read, consider the following questions:

1. What do the authors believe American money has bought in Nicaragua?
2. How in the author's opinion have the *contras* violated Nicaraguan health care programs?
3. What two official US government purposes do the authors believe are served in its attempts to punish the Sandinistas?

Richard J. Barnet and Peter R. Kornbluh, "Reagan's Secret War Against Nicaragua," originally published in the April 18, 1984 issue of *The Los Angeles Times.* Reprinted with permission of the authors.

The Reagan Administration, which has strongly condemned Syria and Iran for promoting state terrorism in the Middle East, has nonetheless made that tactic the mainstay of its so-called secret war against Nicaragua's leftist government. . . .

As a. . .visit to Nicaragua showed, the result of CIA operations there is a U.S.-supported terrorist insurgency that has killed hundreds of civilians, devastated whole communities and increased misery and deprivation by crippling the country's economy.

"The United States has paid for the blood and tears of the Nicaraguan people," Tomás Borge, the Sandinista interior minister told us in Managua. What the American money bought last year according to Nicaraguan government figures, was the death of 300 Sandinista soldiers and the murder of 346 noncombatants, 104 of whom were teachers, health-care workers, agronomists and church officials attempting to bring human services to rural areas.

The Sandinistas believe that the *contras* deliberately target civilians working with the government's rural programs, because, as one Nicaraguan Interior Ministry official explained, "They represent the essence of the revolution." While the regime has been criticized for its authoritarian tendencies since the overthrow of Anastasio Somoza in 1979, it has also been commended for improving living conditions among peasants. According to the World Bank, the government "has given top priority to education" and has conducted "mass vaccination and cleanup campaigns" in impoverished rural areas. Even the U.S. State Department in its 1983 Human Rights report credits the Sandinistas' "efforts to improve health service," citing decreases in diseases such as diarrhea, malaria and polio, and the construction of new health-care centers and hospitals.

The *contras*, however, are attempting to disrupt these programs. To block gains in health-care, for example, they have attempted to dissuade peasants from participating in vaccination drives, calling the medicine "serums of communism." The *contras* have destroyed 22 rural health clinics; 19 medical workers have been killed, including one German doctor and one French. The economic toll on Nicaragua, whose entire national budget, Borge points out, is less than one-sixth the cost of the B-1 bomber program, is equally brutal. The Sandinista government estimates economic damage caused by the counterrevolution at $100 million. Sabotage has taken a variety of forms: Nicaragua's largest petroleum storage tanks at the port of Corinto were destroyed during a machine gun attack from high-speed boats in October, 1983; electrical and communications centers and the international airport in Managua have been damaged in aerial bombing raids; main bridges have been dynamited and dozens of

Clay Bennet, *St. Petersburg Times*, reprinted with permission.

warehouses, construction sites, factory buildings and other facilities burned.

In an effort to block shipping and impede foreign trade, the *contras* have begun to mine Nicaraguan ports. Among the seven ships that have been damaged are Soviet, Japanese and Dutch vessels.

Agriculture is also a target. Government authorities claim a significant percentage of the cotton and coffee crops—Nicaragua's primary cash exports—went unharvested last year because of *contra* attacks. In one small northern village we visited, two men had been hacked to death in December, when they went into the fields to pick their crops. Such attacks have forced an estimated 55,000 peasants to flee their lands, leaving their property and possessions behind and creating additional resettlement costs for the Sandinista regime.

These attacks, coupled with the Reagan Administration's economic sanctions against Nicaragua, have had a major impact on the country's vulnerable economy. The destruction of the petroleum installation in Corinto, for example, forced the Sandinistas to ration gasoline. The loss of export earnings from coffee and cotton has contributed to shortages of basic commodities Nicaragua cannot afford to import. Productivity has been hurt as workers break from their jobs for militia training.

"Increasingly active anti-Sandinista guerrilla movements," acknowledges the 1983 Foreign Economic Trends report issued by the U.S. embassy in Managua, are "among [Nicaragua's] chronic economic problems for which there is no early solution in view."

Change and America's Backyard

It is not Cuban infrastructure, "interdiction" of arms or a concern for democracy as U.S. officials have alleged, that account for the Administration's conduct in Nicaragua. Rather, like so many of his predecessors, President Reagan seems driven to control the process of internal change in America's "backyard." "We set the limits of diversity," Henry Kissinger once told a group of officials during a strategy meeting on how to destabilize the Allende government in Chile, and that is what the Reagan Administration is intent on now doing in Nicaragua.

Since the *contras'* tactics are unlikely to produce democracy, one must conclude the Administration is using them to punish the Sandinistas. This punishment serves two purposes:

First, the pain and damage the *contras* inflict on the Nicaraguan people and the economy sends a chilling message to other revolutionary movements in the region that a challenge to U.S. influence will be met with prolonged and unyielding hostility.

Second, U.S. policy-makers harbor the illusion that the combination of an unending war of attrition and increasing economic pressures will change the political climate and erode public support for the Nicaraguan government, thereby forcing the Sandinistas to concede the basic principles of their revolution.

But as ardent nationalists, the Sandinistas are not about to capitulate. "It is a false premise that more pressure will bring more concession until we make the concession they want—the revolution," Borge told us. "It is impossible that we are going to reverse everything, let the National Guard come back, become a satellite of the United States again. They are wasting their time if they think we will make those types of concessions."

Moreover, just as the Sandinistas derived inspiration from Augusto Sandino, who resisted American Marines in the late 1920s and early 1930s, it is prudent to assume that nationalist resistance to current U.S. policy will inspire another generation of Nicaraguans and other Central Americans. Nationalism, a phenomenon U.S. policy-makers have never understood but have done much to further, will prove to be more readily exportable than either revolution or counterrevolution.

Promoting counterrevolutionary violence is also a dangerous policy. Not only has the Reagan Administration legitimized terrorism and subversion—sending a message of endorsement to right-wing death-squads throughout the region and undercutting its opposition to terrorism elsewhere—it is also undermining the real U.S. national interests of peace and stability in the region. The *contras'* war has already claimed hundreds of lives, and it threatens to claim many more.

US Nicaraguan Involvement Immoral

It's hypocritical, too, to talk of forcing dictatorships down the throats of peoples most of whose history has been a tale of oppression, at a time when counterrevolutionaries armed, trained and directed by the U.S. are trying to force their own U.S.-supplied power down the throats of Nicaraguans. You can't shoot your way into power in El Salvador, as Reaganspeak would have it, but it's all right in Nicaragua. . . .

More than moral and legal considerations are involved in all this. The touchy situation between Nicaragua and Honduras, which shelters the C.I.A.-backed contras, could touch off a Central American war; or, if the contras were to succeed in overthrowing the Government, the Sandinistas would take to the hills with the support of most Nicaraguans. A long and bloody civil war would surely result. The United States, in either event, inevitably would be drawn in on what most of Latin America would see as the wrong side.

And anyone who takes that prospect lightly would do well to remember that for five years after 1926, in the formidable mountains and jungles of Nicaragua, the U.S. Marines tried to defeat a handful of guerrillas led by the original Sandino. They never did.

Tom Wicker, *The New York Times,* April 20, 1984.

It is becoming more likely that these will be American lives. Already one U.S. army pilot, Jeffrey Schwab, whose helicopter deliberately or accidently entered Nicaraguan airspace on the Honduran border on Jan. 14, has died. With U.S. troops now based in Honduras and the role of American military advisers in El Salvador expanding, the danger grows that the Reagan Administration may involve the United States in a regional conflagration. Moreover, this war threatens to escalate into real East-West conflict. The damage to the Soviet oil tanker and injury to five of its crewmen last month by a U.S.-supplied mine demonstrates that the United States' covert intervention in Nicaragua could trigger a serious increase in Soviet-American tension and under certain circumstances actual confrontation.

The future of this war depends on continued U.S. support, for the *contras* cannot survive without it. As the Administration seeks to spend $21 million more to fund its surrogates, the public and its Congress ought to ask: Are the *contras* the type of allies we can afford? Does protracted terror and violence serve U.S. interests in Central America?

We might wonder, as Will Rogers did over half a century ago when 5,000 U.S. Marines were engaged in a futile campaign to eliminate Augusto Sandino's guerrilla army: "Why are we in Nicaragua, and what the hell are we doing there?"

Contra War Affects Civil Liberties

The *contra* war has exacerbated the political tensions between the revolutionary government and its domestic opposition. After U.S.-trained saboteurs dynamited two main bridges in the north in March, 1982, the Sandinistas clamped down on their critics. A state of emergency was declared; press censorship was imposed and the activities of opposition unions and political parties were curtailed.

The Nicaraguan Revolution has learned, as one Foreign Ministry official put it, "an extremely valuable and important lesson" from Chile, where between 1970 and 1973 the CIA funneled $8 million dollars to opposition newspapers, unions and political parties in a successful bid to destabilize the elected socialist government of Salvador Allende. The Sandinistas are aware that on March 9, 1981, six weeks after his inauguration, President Reagan authorized CIA funding of anti-Sandinista political and private economic interests in Nicaragua, and they do not intend to suffer Allende's fate.

Thus, for the opposition leaders who have "chosen to stay and fight," in the words of Enrique Bolaños, head of the most prominent private-sector organization, COSEP, U.S. covert activities are the kiss of death. Although critics of the Sandinistas vocally support U.S. pressure on the regime as a method to moderate the leftist direction of the revolution, CIA intervention, as Kissinger commission member Carlos Diáz-Alejandro, a Yale economist, noted, "is used by Managua to brand all dissidents as pawns of a foreign power, eroding the legitimacy of all dissidence within Nicaragua."

Contra Groups Explained

Although President Reagan calls them "freedom fighters," and they call themselves "commandos of liberty," the *contras'* leaders have few democratic credentials. To be sure, several prominent members, most notably Eden Pastora and Alfonso Robelo, are disenchanted former officials of the Sandinista government. But their Costa Rica-based organization, the Revolutionary Democratic Alliance, is small and until recently has not been the major recipient of the Reagan Administration's largess.

By far the largest and most active *contra* group—and the one most closely allied with the United States—is the Nicaraguan Democratic Force (FDN). Forged with the help of the CIA in 1981 from several smaller *contra* organizations, the FDN's seven-member directorate includes Somoza's former vice president and a brigadier general from his praetorian guard, the Nicaraguan National Guard. The FDN's miltary staff, and many of its field commanders, were formerly sergeants and colonels in the guard, which has lent credence to the Sandinista charge that the *contras* are *Somocistas* attempting to regain power.

No to American Imperialism

The Reagan Administration is adding another ignominious chapter to the long history of United States intervention and counterrevolutionary subversion in Central and South America. Increasingly aware that the insurgents in El Salvador cannot be defeated by a poorly motivated army and a business-military oligarchy with little or no control over death squads that have kill-ed thousands of innocent Salvadorans, the White House and the Pentagon have evidently decided that a large part of the solution to this and other related problems in Central America lies in the overthrow of the Nicaraguan government. The Reagan Administration's strategy rests on the premise that the overthrow of the Sandinists by ex-Somocista National Guardsmen will bring about the establishment of a "democratic" but strongly anti-Communist regime in Managua. With the Sandinists out of the way, the rebel forces in El Salvador, deprived of their main source of arms, would be compelled to accept "free" elections on American terms. But the real thrust of this strategy, even more than anti-Sandinist, appears to be anti-Soviet and anti-Cuban. President Reagan persists in ascribing the political and social aspirations of the Sandinists and the fighting will of guerrillas in El Salvador to Soviet and Cuban plots. Such reasoning is, in our view, as simplistic as it is deceitful. It is also dangerous and threatens to extend, not limit, military conflict in Central America.

Policy Statement of CUNY, Committee Against US Intervention in Latin America.

The FDN rank and file, variously estimated at 5,000 to 7,000 men, is made up of former guardsmen who fled Nicaragua after the revolution, Miskito Indians whom the Sandinistas alienated by trying to coerce their integration into the revolution and small landowners and peasants who have been disaffected for religious or ideological reasons.

In their recruitment drive, the *contras* have appealed to the "traditional values" of rural Nicaraguans. Their propaganda, dropped from airplanes over northern Nicaraguan villages along with plastic bags filled with candy, balloons and soaps, depicts the hand of the FDN offering a basket filled with gifts, a cross and the Nicaraguan flag. Religious freedom and the fight against "Soviet imperialism" are central themes of the counterrevolution. "All Christian Nicaraguans are obliged to fight against the atheist Sandinista government," the *contra* literature asserts. . . .

Revenge against the Sandinistas and their supporters appears to be a major motive of the contras' campaign. Some insurgent leaders have threatened a blood bath if they are successful: "Come the counterrevolution there will be a massacre in Nicaragua," one promised a *Newsweek* reporter in Honduras. "We have a lot of scores to settle. There will be bodies from the [Honduran] border to Managua."

But after more than two years of CIA planning and training, and massive injections of American money, the *contras* have proven an ineffective guerrilla army, unable to accomplish even their short-term goal of seizing territory and declaring a "liberated zone." Last September, CIA advisers in Honduras reportedly directed the *contras* to shift from a "war of position" to a "war of attrition" and concentrate on commando-style sabotage operations rather than risk heavy casualties in confrontations with the Sandinista army. But even though they have since launched a series of successful air and sea attacks on port cities and economic facilities, CIA analysts do not believe the *contras* have the military capacity or political sophistication to do more than wreak havoc and terror throughout Nicaragua. . . .

"Right wing violence undercuts the Salvadoran Government's military and political efforts and ultimately makes its struggle with the left unwinnable."

The Death Squads Discredit US Involvement

Richard L. Millett

Richard L. Millett is the author of *Guardians of the Dynasty* and *The Restless Caribbean*. The following viewpoint is taken from an article that appeared in *The New York Times*. In it, Mr. Millett discusses the issue of death squads and argues that they are a blight on the US conscience. He feels that the US must make verifiable sanctions against the El Salvador government to stop them.

As you read, consider the following questions:

1. Why does Mr. Millett feel that past US attempts to end the violent death squads have failed?
2. What four steps are necessary to end the death squads, in the author's opinion?

Richard L. Millett, "To Stop Death Squads," *The New York Times*, December 27, 1983. Copyright © 1983/84 by The New York Times Company. Reprinted by permission.

Can the United States stop death squad activity in El Salvador? Do we have the leverage to do so? These are the questions raised by Washington's recent criticism of the death squads. Certainly, it would require more than words to eliminate their violence: What's needed are difficult, concrete actions, involving major risks for both Washington and San Salvador.

A chorus of Administration officials has denounced the death squads. Deputy Secretary of State Kenneth Dam characterized them as "enemies of democracy every bit as much as the guerrillas and their Cuban and Soviet sponsors," while Vice President Bush warned that continued death squad murders would result in the loss of United States support. El Salvador's armed forces have joined in these condemnations, declaring that death squads actually aid the guerrillas and proclaiming a determination to fight the squads until they "disappear forever."

These denunciations are significant, but the death squads have had no difficulty surviving previous rhetorical attacks. From time to time, they have curtailed their activities in response to United States criticism, but the groups themselves and the network that supports them have remained intact, ready for revival whenever the extreme right felt that the times were propitious.

The death squads are more a symptom than a cause of El Salvador's problems. Political violence is long familiar to the region. In the 1930's, the military killed 20,000 suspects as part of a campaign to eliminate a few hundred Communists. Today, this attitude persists, expressed in the right-wing slogan that it is better to prevent than to cure, meaning that it is preferable to kill a potential subversive than to give him an opportunity to take up arms.

No Trials or Convictions

Such attitudes, combined with the privileged position of El Salvador's military, help explain why no officer or prominent civilian has ever been tried, much less convicted, for killing suspected leftists. Any judge or prosecuting attorney who publicly contemplated such action would be identified as a leftist sympathizer—and would face the obvious consequences.

Can the United States do anything about this? Many Salvadorans find it hard to take Washington's pronouncements on right-wing violence seriously. True, President Jimmy Carter cut off our aid in December 1980 in response to right-wing violence. But Salvadorans recall the speed with which he resumed and even increased aid in January 1981 when the left launched a major offensive. They also point to President Reagan's veto of the legislation making Presidential certification of human rights progress in El Salvador a condition for continuing aid and to his unsubstantiated speculations concerning possi-

Berry's World

"I feel like a prostitute, curbing the death squads just so we can get American arms!"

© 1983 by NEA, Inc.

ble left-wing involvement in death squad killings. To many Salvadorans, this is evidence that Washington's attacks on their human rights abuses are designed for domestic consumption and are not to be taken too seriously.

Cosmetic Changes

Many on the Salvadoran right also believe that United States critics can be mollified by a few cosmetic changes. In this, too, the Salvadorans have learned from past experience. All that is required, they believe, is that the level of violence should drop for a while, a few officers should be transferred or retired (or, in extreme cases, arrested and charged, but never actually tried) and that the Government give ritual assent to the need to end violence on both the left and the right.

Certainly, that is all that can be expected from San Salvador if it perceives that, once again, Washington's objections are largely political—designed to mollify domestic critics, counter Congressional cuts in aid appropriations or forestall divisions in the Kissinger commission. The result will be that the basic system that produced and nourished the death squads will survive virtually unchanged.

Things could be different, however, if—and only if—the President has finally understood that right-wing violence undercuts the Salvadoran Government's military and political efforts and ultimately makes its struggle with the left unwinnable. If that is true, the Administration may now be committed to firm action to force Salvadoran authorities to prevent right-wing violence and prosecute those responsible for some of the murders of recent years, notably those involving agricultural advisers and churchwomen from the United States.

Breaking the grip of the death squads and purging their supporters from positions of power would require four basic conditions:

Four Conditions Needed

First, there must be clear evidence of Washington's will and determination to effect such changes. The Administration must make clear that such reform is an absolute necessity, not simply a desirable outcome. This must become the primary focus of dealings with the Salvadoran Government and military—not just a rider attached to other policies for political reasons.

Second, this attitude must be communicated firmly and consistently by all sectors of the Administration and their supporters. All remarks from Washington must make clear that this is our first priority—more important even than curbing perceived Cuban influence in Central America.

The third prerequisite is patience and perserverance. Elimination of the death squads will not come easily, and Salvadoran authorities will try every possible subterfuge. The social and political conditions that produced them are the products of centuries of injustice and repression. They cannot be dismantled in a few months.

Finally, ending the death squads' reign of terror would require a willingness to take serious risks. It must be clear to the Salvadoran military that the United States is prepared to cut or suspend its aid, risking significant military successes by the far left. This risk is very real, but the risks posed by the death squads are even greater.

It must be repeatedly and publicly stated—and, if possible, incorporated into binding legislation—that El Salvador will lose United States support if its right-wing violence continues unabated. Admittedly, such a policy would reduce the United States' flexibility and would open opportunities for the left. But Washington's credibility on this issue has been so severely damaged by past actions that nothing less would have the necessary credibility.

The Administration's actions have yet to measure up to its rhetoric. Its words indicate a growing commitment to curbing death squad activities, but serious questions remain about its unity, patience and willingness to take risks. At this critical moment, such partial commitments are a recipe for ultimate disaster.

"El Salvador is resorting to counter-terror because the alternative they have been offered is permanent war."

The Death Squads Are Not a Moral Issue

Patrick J. Buchanan

Patrick J. Buchanan is a syndicated columnist and commentator on the NBC radio network. He has an A.B. in English and a M.S. in journalism. From 1966-1974, he served as executive assistant to Richard Nixon and as special assistant and consultant to Presidents Nixon and Ford. He is the author of *Conservative Votes, Liberal Victories* and *The New Majority.* In the following viewpoint, Mr. Buchanan believes that if the US were to take sanctions against the Salvadoran government for death squad activity, it would only hasten guerrilla takeover in the area.

As you read, consider the following questions:

1. Why does Mr. Buchanan believe linking US aid to El Salvador with human rights is wrong?
2. Why, in the author's opinion, are right-wing death squads being unjustifiably attacked?

Patrick J. Buchanan, "Liberals Abhor Only Right-Wing Death Squads," *Human Events,* February 11, 1984. Reprinted by permission of Tribune Media Services Inc.

The enemies of Mr. Reagan's Central American policy have seized upon the most promising tactic yet:

Exploit American revulsion at the "right-wing death squads" and bring about termination of U.S. military aid to the government that cannot, or will not, control them.

A cutoff in weapons to El Salvador would, of course, bring about the objective the Communists seek, an objective their *de facto* allies in American politics and press are quite willing to accept: an end to the bloody war through imposition of a Sandinista-style regime.

Correctly, Henry Kissinger refused to sign on to his commission's recommendation to terminate aid, if the regime does not control the death squads. Such a decision, Kissinger noted, would be absurd; it would lead to a Marxist victory, a strategic defeat for the United States, a permanent human rights disaster for El Salvador.

What Kissinger did not say was that none of the above would greatly trouble the American Left, which has found in these death squads its excuse, its rationale, for doing what the Left has long wanted to do—scuttle and run from Central America, and watch from a distance, Pontius-Pilate like, as the right-wing regimes in El Salvador, Guatemala and Honduras are carved up by Castroite guerrillas.

Distinguishing Friends from Enemies

Watching those Democratic candidates debating in New Hampshire recently competing with one another as to who would be more hostile toward South Africa, who would be more forthcoming toward Fidel Castro, one realizes most of them have lost the essential quality for leadership of a Great Power. They cannot distinguish flawed friends from mortal enemies; they have contracted the Carthaginian disease.

Watching these public displays of rage, revulsion and horror at the murderous deeds of the "right-wing death squads," it is hard to escape the conclusion that it is their political orientation the Left finds repelling.

During the Nicaraguan Revolution, for example, one of Somoza's trusted generals was lured into a honey trap, mutilated horribly and murdered. The siren who lured the general into the hands of that death squad was Nora Astorga. Subsequently, she was feted in the Washington liberal press as a heroine of the Revolution.

The PLO's death squads which have operated all over Europe and the Middle East do not seem to have diminished that organization's claim to be the "legitimate representative" of the Palestinian people.

When Fidel Castro was putting enemies up against the wall

and executing them without trial, it did not seem to diminish greatly his appeal as an "existential hero" to the Left. When that bomb was recently exploded in South Africa, killing several and injuring scores of people, did anyone contend this permanently discredited the African National Congress which claimed credit?

"Death Squads" is a term reserved for those who kill in the cause of saving a centrist or right-wing regime. If you wish a general absolution for murder in this modern age, you must explain that you are killing "reactionaries" to advance the people's revolution.

The most successful tactic, for example, of the guerrillas in El Salvador is to use the element of surprise, shoot the peasant-soldiers guarding some installation or village, execute the local officials supporting the government, propagandize the peasants, and move on.

Murder Considered Normal

The shooting of soldiers and the execution of government sympathizers is considered normal in a revolution; it becomes cold-blooded murder when government troops retaliate in kind, shooting soldiers and executing sympathizers of the revolution.

Watching how Gen. Somoza fared in neighboring Nicaragua, the Salvadorans have apparently decided to ignore the advice of

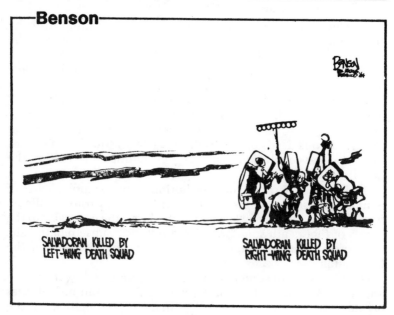

Reprinted by permission: Tribune Media Services, Inc.

America and follow the example of Argentina.

Faced with rising urban terror in 1976, the Argentina military seized power and waged a war of counter-terror. With military and police and free-lance operators, between 6,000 and 15,000 leftists disappeared. Brutal, yes; also successful. Today, peace reigns in Argentina, security has been restored; the generals have given way, temporarily, to civilian democratic rule.

El Salvador, I suspect, is ignoring America's outbursts and pursuing a strategy of counter-terror, because America's policy—neither the President's nor Dr. Kissinger's—offers no light at the end of the tunnel. There is no date certain, after which the Communists will be killed or routed, the base camp of subversion in Nicaragua will be dismantled and pacified.

El Salvador is resorting to counter-terror because the alternative they have been offered is permanent war.

Oddly, the President who used to quote Gen. MacArthur so often that in war there is no substitute for victory, has not yet offered a strategy for victory.

a basic reading and thinking skill

The Ability to Empathize

The ability to empathize, to see life and experience its joys and problems through another person's eyes and feelings, is a helpful skill to acquire if one is the learn from the life situations of others.

Consider the following example:

Salvadoran Refugee Seeks Sanctuary

You want to know why I left Salvador? Because it was too dangerous to ride the bus anymore. Really, that's the truth. I hope maybe to return someday, but you don't know how bad it is over there. You know, I actually once saw a dog with a human hand in his mouth walking through the village near mine.

Here's what happened to me. I used to take the bus into town from my village every day. But half of the time I never arrived. Between the guerrillas and the security forces. . . .One day the *campesinos* would hijack the bus and use it for a roadblock, or else they'd make everybody get out and they'd throw a bomb inside the bus—just to destroy it and disrupt the transportation. Another day the National Guard would stop the bus and spend hours looking at everybody's papers and searching the suspicious ones. . . .

I was a little nervous when I got on the bus in the morning, hoping that nothing was going to happen. The bus was pretty crowded as usual, and one of the passengers was a short policeman with an automatic rifle. . . .

At one stop a young man came on the bus, about eighteen. He was wearing a clean shirt and clean trousers, but you could tell by his shoes and his skin that he was pretty poor. I guessed he was going into town to look for a job. He was really tall, that's why I noticed him so much. You could see his head above everybody else's. When he got on, he was pressed by the crowd up against the policeman. The young man apologized a couple of times, but I could tell that the policeman was getting irritated.

Then I heard the policeman say, "Hey! Bastard! You're stealing all my oxygen up there!" The young man looked down at the policeman and he laughed like it had been a joke and he was being polite. He actually thought that the policeman was being funny. Then the policeman yelled again, and said that the guy was laughing at him. He told the bus driver to stop. He made the boy get down from the bus. And then—I swear it, this happened in front of me—he shot him. Shot him twice in the head. . . Then he got back on the bus, and he told the bus driver to continue. The policeman took a deep breath, and laughed a little bit, and said "Ah, yes, that's much better now." As we drove away, I looked out the window and saw the boy's body, his clean clothes all splattered with blood. . . .

Tomorrow, I thought, it could happen to me. That's when I decided to leave Salvador and come here. I couldn't get papers, so I sneaked across the border. I almost died walking across the desert. Now I am safe. I hope I can stay here until the war is over, if the immigration people here don't catch me.

Michel J. Englebert, *The Progressive*, March 1983.

Instructions:

Part 1

The class should break into groups of six, read the above selection, and discuss the following situation:

Assume that the man above is seeking sanctuary in your church. Churches in America have been providing sanctuary even though it violates immigration laws. Your church is debating whether or not to give this man sanctuary and put itself in conflict with the federal government. Your small group should act as the church board, trying to decide whether or not to provide sanctuary. When deciding, think about the issues involved and discuss how the following individuals would react in this situation. What reasons might they give for their actions? Try to imagine and explain their feelings.

the man in the example

US immigration officials

a member of the church against sanctuary

author of viewpoint 3 in this chapter

author of viewpoint 6 in this chapter

yourself

Part 2

After your group comes to a decision on the issue of sanctuary, prepare a written rationale to present before your congregation in which you explain why you came to your decision.

Periodical Bibliography

The following list of periodical articles deals with the subject matter of this chapter.

Elliot Abrams — "The Situation We Face in Central America," *Vital Speeches of the Day*, December 1, 1982.

James Chance — "Choices on Salvador," *The New York Times*, November 27, 1983.

Christopher Dickey — "Behind the Death Squads," *National Review*, December 26, 1983.

Congressional Digest — "Central American Policy," October 1983.

Thomas O. Enders — "U.S. Strategy in Central America," *Department of State Bulletin*, June 1983.

Carolyn Forche and Leonel Gomez — "The Military's Web of Corruption," *The Nation*, October 23, 1982.

Nicolas Goldberg — "Don't Aid Central American Police," *The New York Times*, February 23, 1984.

Stephen Kinzer — "Nicaragua: The Beleaguered Revolution," *New York Times Magazine*, August 23, 1983.

New Guard — Summer 1981, "Why We Must Aid El Salvador," Special Issue.

Newsweek — "Attacking the Death Squads," January 16, 1984.

Orville H. Schell — "Salvadoran Slaughter," *The New York Times*, April 14, 1984.

William Stief — "Voices from Nicaragua," *The Progressive*, May 1982.

Nancy Strogoff — "Nicaragua: The Other War," *The Progressive*, January 1984.

Meldrim Thomson — "Policy for Survival: New Monroe Doctrine," *Conservative Digest*, June 1983.

Richard H. Ullman — "At War with Nicaragua," *Foreign Affairs*, Fall 1983.

Pete Wilson — "Central America, Turmoil at America's Doorstep," *Vital Speeches of the Day*, October 15, 1983.

Why Is Central America a Conflict Area?

"If Central America were not racked with poverty, there would be no revolution."

Poverty Is the Cause of Conflict

Christopher J. Dodd

Christopher J. Dodd is a Democratic US senator from Connecticut. He earned a B.A. from Providence College and a J.D. from the University of Louisville. During 1966-1968, he served as a volunteer in the Peace Corps in the Dominican Republic. In the following viewpoint, Senator Dodd declares that the revolutionary movements in Central America are indigenous in nature and spurred by massive poverty in the area.

As you read, consider the following questions:

1. What are the four ideas Mr. Dodd claims all Americans will agree on?
2. What has US military assistance accomplished in Central America, in the author's opinion?

Christopher J. Dodd, in an address given in Washington, DC on April 27, 1983.

We as a nation have learned painfully that the truth is never as simple as some would paint it. Charts and statistics can be used or misused to prove any side of a case. And speeches can sound very good without being very right.

So first of all, let me state clearly that on some very important things, all Americans stand in agreement.

We will oppose the establishment of Marxist states in Central America.

We will not accept to see the creation of Soviet military bases in Central America.

And, we will not tolerate the placement of Soviet offensive missiles in Central America—or anywhere in this hemisphere.

Finally, we are fully prepared to defend our security and the security of the Americas, if necessary, by military means.

All patriotic Americans share these goals. But many of us in Congress, Democrats and Republicans, disagree with the President because we believe the means he has chosen will not fulfill them.

Those of us who oppose the President's policy believe that he is mistaken in critical ways. To begin with, we believe the Administration fundamentally misunderstands the causes of conflict in Central America. We cannot afford to found so important a policy on ignorance—and the painful truth is that many of our highest officials seem to know as little about Central America in 1983 as we knew about Indochina in 1963.

I've lived with the people in this region. Let me share some facts with you about Central America.

Most of the people there are appallingly poor. They can't afford to feed their families when they're hungry. They can't find a doctor for them when they're sick. They live in rural shacks with dirt floors or city slums without plumbing or clean water. The majority can't read or write; and many of them can't even count.

It takes all five Spanish-speaking countries of Central America more than a year to provide what this nation does, or produce what this nation does, in less than three days. Virtually none of even that meager amount ever reaches the bulk of the people. In short, a very few live in isolated splendor while the very many suffer in shantytown squalor. In country after country, dictatorship or military dominance has stifled democracy and destroyed human rights.

Poverty and Revolution

If Central America were not racked with poverty, there would be no revolution. If Central America were not racked with hunger, there would be no revolution. If Central America were not racked with injustice, there would be no revolution. In short, there would be nothing for the Soviets to exploit. But unless those oppressive conditions change, the region will continue to seethe with revolution—with or without the Soviets.

Instead of trying to do something about the factions or factors which breed revolution, this Administration has turned to massive military buildups at a cost of hundreds of millions of dollars. Its policy is ever-increasing military assistance, endless military training, and further military involvement. This is a formula for failure. And it is a proven prescription for picking a loser. The American people know that we have been down this road before—and that it only leads to a dark tunnel of endless intervention.

Real Enemy Is Poverty

I am proud to join you in opposition to an absurd policy of intervention in a country where the real enemies of the people are hunger, poverty, unemployment and repression. . . .

The people of El Salvador are desperately poor. The infant mortality rate is four times that of the United States. Functional illiteracy is over 90 percent. . . .

A legitimate government protects the interests of the people; it does not destroy them. Legitimate government uses the military to defend the country from foreign attack—not kill more of its own population in order to maintain the wealth of the few thousand descendants of the "Fourteen Families" who have owned El Salvador in the Twentieth Century.

James Oberstar, in a speech delivered on April 11, 1983, in Virginia, Minnesota.

The President himself told us that things were not going well in Central America. But for this the President cannot blame Congress. We have given him what he has asked for. Seven hundred million in economic and military assistance has been delivered or is on its way to El Salvador since Ronald Reagan came to office, all at his request and all with Congressional approval. One of every five Salvadoran soldiers fighting for its government was trained right here in the United States. American soldiers are there now training Salvadoran army units which are employing modern weapons built in American factories.

The President asks for an even greater commitment. His requests for El Salvador alone will bring the total aid to that country during his term to more than $1 billion.

One billion dollars to counter a rebel army that, according to all reports, does not exceed 7,000 guerrillas.

That means you are paying $140,000 in hard-earned tax dollars for each one of those guerrillas we are trying to defeat.

While your tax dollars have been pouring into El Salvador, the money skimmed off by that nation's very rich is leaving the country. For every dollar we've sent in, more than a dollar has gone out—to numbered accounts in Zurich or to buy stocks on Wall Street. It raises the question of why we should invest in the future of El Salvador when the wealthiest citizens of that country are investing in Swiss banks.

What return have we received for all we have spent? The army in El Salvador has been reluctant to fight—and is led by an officer corps working a nine-to-five shift with weekends off. Land reform has been abandoned. At least 30,000 civilians have been killed and the majority of them have been victims of the Government's own security forces. American nuns and labor advisors have been murdered—and the judicial system is so intimidated that it cannot even bring accused murderers to trial.

For those 30,000 murders, confirmed by our own Embassy, there have been fewer than 200 convictions.

American dollars alone cannot buy military victory—that is the lesson of the painful past and of this newest conflict in Central America. If we continue down that road, if we continue to ally ourselves with repression, we will not only deny our own most basic values, we will also find ourselves once again on the losing side. It is folly, pure and simple, to pursue a course which is wrong in principle—in order to wage a conflict which cannot be won.

After 30,000 deaths, after hundreds of millions of dollars, with the ante going up, with no end in sight, with no hope for any change, real change, the time has come for a different approach. Yes, we are fully prepared to be involved in Central America. But the question is the nature and quality of our involvement. We must offer an alternative policy that can work.

Components of an Alternative Policy

First, we should use the power and influence of the United States to achieve an immediate cessation of hostilities in both El Salvador and Nicaragua. Already in both countries too many people have died. It is time for the killing to stop.

Second, the United States should use all its power and influence to work for a negotiated political settlement in Central America.

In El Salvador, the rebels have offered to negotiate unconditionally. Let us test their sincerity. We certainly have the leverage to move the Government to the bargaining table. On his recent trip to that very Catholic region, the Pope lent the moral force of his office to such a step. It is practical and realistic to expect, that if we support it, these talks can get underway. And

every major ally of ours in the region—Mexico, Panama, Venezuela, and Colombia—is anxious for such a step to be taken and has offered, I might add, to make the arrangements.

Those same nations have volunteered to bring Nicaragua into negotiations—and Nicaragua has agreed to talk. Instead, as we know from the present accounts, press accounts, this Administration is conducting a not-so-secret war inside that country.

No one in this Congress or this country is under the delusion that the Sandinista government is a model democracy or a force for stability. But the insurgents we have supported are the remnants of the old Somoza regime—a regime whose corruption, graft, torture, and despotism made it universally despised in Nicaragua. The Sandinistas may not be winners, but right now we are backing sure losers. We are doing for the Sandinista Marxists what they could not do for themselves. We are weakening the very groups inside Nicaragua which believe in a free and democratic society. And that is the sad irony of this Administration's policy.

Third, we must restore America's role as a source of hope and a force for progress in Central America. We must help governments only if they will help their own people. We must hear the cry for bread, and schools, work, and opportunity that comes from campesinos everywhere in this hemisphere. We must make violent revolution preventable by making peaceful revolution possible.

Considering History

Most important, this approach would permit the United States to move with the tide of history rather than stand against it.

For us, the stakes are diplomatic, political, and strategic. But for the people of El Salvador, life itself is on the line.

I have been to that country and I know about the morticians who travel the streets each morning to collect the bodies of those summarily dispatched the night before by Salvadoran security forces—gangland-style—the victim, a person on a bended knee, thumbs wired behind their back, a bullet through the brain.

We recoil at such an image, for our association with criminals such as these is not America's tradition. In other, brighter days we have stood for the aspirations of all of the people who are part of the Americas. Two centuries ago, our nation raised the light of liberty before the world—and all of this hemisphere looked to us as an example and an inspiration. In this Capitol building, from which I speak tonight, men like Daniel Webster, Henry Clay, Abraham Lincoln once spoke of an America leading the world to progress and human rights—and people everywhere listened with hope to those words.

There is no greater or larger ideal than the one which was forged here in the early days of this Republic. That ideal of liberty is our greatest strength as a nation; it is a powerful and peaceful weapon against tyranny of any kind anywhere in this hemisphere.

We can take the road of military escalation. But the real—what

102

we really don't know—what the next step will be, where it will lead or how much it will cost.

This much, however, we do know. It will mean greater violence. It will mean greater bloodshed. It will mean greater hostilities. And, inevitably, the day will come when it will mean a regional conflict in Central America.

When that day comes—when the "dogs of war" are loose in Central America, when the cheering has stopped—we will know where the President's appeal for more American money and a deeper American commitment has taken us. Thank you, and good night.

"Poverty. . .is not what has produced or what sustains the current crisis and war."

Poverty Is Not the Cause of Conflict

Max Singer

Max Singer is well known as the author of *Nicaragua: The Stolen Revolution*, a book that documents his view that the Sandinista government has not fulfilled its promise to the Nicaraguan people and has instead become a communist puppet regime. In the following viewpoint, Mr. Singer speaks out regarding the economic conditions in Central America declaring that although poverty is widespread in the region, it is not the cause of the existing conflict.

As you read, consider the following questions:

1. What statistics does the author quote to prove his stance that Central America's economy is flourishing?
2. What does the author believe the revolutionaries are fighting for?

Max Singer, "Poverty and Injustice Not the Cause of Fighting in Central America," *The Union Leader*, April 5, 1984. Reprinted with permission.

While the countries of Central America are still poor, and have unequal income distributions, the primary cause of the current conflict is not economic, social, or political injustice; the current conflict results from an attempt by small groups of ideological extremists to take power—from successful pro-democratic revolutions.

During the years between 1960 and the revolutions of 1979, average incomes in Nicaragua and El Salvador had been growing at about 2 percent per year (the same rate U.S. incomes grew during our advance from poverty in the 1800s). Infant mortality had been declining fast (down almost one half in El Salvador and over one-third in Nicaragua). Health had been improving rapidly (life expectancy up 12 years in El Salvador and nine years in Nicaragua). The proportion of children in school was going up (to over 26 percent in secondary school in both El Salvador and Nicaragua—compared to only 13 percent and 7 percent in 1960).

In 1979 this social progress was joined by political progress with the ending of dictatorships or military governments in El Salvador and Nicaragua, as well as in Honduras (which had also seen substantial social and economic progress).

It was after these two decades of progress that the current counter-revolutionary conflict began with Sandinista seizure of power in 1979 (not from Somoza but from the Sandinistas' allies in the revolution against Somoza) and the formation in 1980 of a guerrilla army to attack the Revolutionary Governing Junta (JRG) in El Salvador. The extremists needed to prevent the success of the moderate revolutions for social justice that had been made by groups committed to democracy.

Social Progress Irrelevant

The extremists against whom the U.S. is fighting are not driven by the need to achieve social progress. They are fighting for sectarian power (although they know that their fight for power sets back social progress). They do not represent the people. Since their actions came after the real revolution they came too late to be "historically inevitable." They have been effective not because of their popularity or the justice of their cause but because they have massive and expert help from outside. (Cuba has more than 10 times as many people in Nicaragua as we have in El Salvador.)

Other countries where the poverty and injustice is worse, and progress slower or not yet really begun, do not have such violent conflict. Therefore, while it is undoubtedly true that poverty is a significant fact in Central America, it is not what has produced or what sustains the current crisis and war.

Working against poverty and injustice, while it is desirable, is not a useful way to deal with the current violent conflict. The opposite approach is more realistic. Instead of solving the conflict by dealing with injustice, it is necessary to deal with injustice by solving the conflict. The necessary first step to substantial economic, social, or human rights progress in El Salvador is to end the war.

Since the "hearts and minds" of the great majority of the people have already rejected the guerrillas—despite the crimes of some government supporters and Army officers—the only way to end the war in El Salvador is to defeat the guerrillas. The guerrillas must be defeated because they are murderous, unpopular, present no just claim, and cannot be satisfied except with complete power.

Political Conditions, Not Poverty Cause Revolution

Here in Latin America, neither social injustice nor poverty has been the fundamental cause of our revolutions. When there has been political violence, and there has been a lot, it involves movements trying to break the iron ring of dictatorial oppression—not economic but political conditions that block access to power.

If the direct cause of the violence in Latin America were social injustice, El Salvador and Guatemala would hardly be the only countries where guerrillas threaten the Governments: We can all think of several other Latin American nations with masses of poor people—countries that, according to the myth, should be excellent candidates for wars of hunger. In fact, however, some of the most violent and fervent revolutions in Latin America occurred in countries that were traditionally considered among the richest in the area—Cuba and Argentina, for example.

Luís Burstin, *The New York Times*, February 9, 1984.

There is much experience to indicate that those who don't try to gain a victory for the democratic side, who sit on the fence or devote their efforts to seeking a non-existent "middle way," will turn out to have helped to bring about an extension of totalitarianism and a defeat for human rights.

Idealistic Americans should be urging our government much more strongly to support the democratic side in the life-or-death struggle for human rights in Central America. A victory for the FMLN and the FLSN is likely in a few years to bring human rights in Central America to as low a level as human rights in Eastern Europe.

"The Soviet Union and Cuba are exploiting the serious problems of very vulnerable Central American societies."

Cuba Is Responsible for the Conflict

Carl Gershman

Carl Gershman is counselor to the US permanent Representative to the United Nations. He graduated magna cum laude from Yale and received his M.Ed. from Harvard. Mr. Gershman is a frequent contributor to several magazines including *Commentary, Spectator, New Leader,* and *The New York Times Magazine* and the author of *The Foreign Policy of American Labor* and co-editor of *Israel, The Arabs, and the Middle East.* In the following viewpoint, Mr. Gershman traces the involvement of Cuba in Central America and concludes that Soviet-backed Cuba is behind the Central American conflict.

As you read, consider the following questions:

1. What strategy in the author's opinion does Cuba use to create revolution in Central America?
2. How was Nicaraguan revolution exported to El Salvador, according to the author?
3. What effect does the author believe has "the armed assault on Central America" had on the US?

Carl Gershman, "Soviet Power in Central America and the Caribbean," *Catholicism in Crisis,* April 1984. Reprinted with permission.

The significance to the United States of developments in Central America and the Caribbean Basin cannot be appreciated apart from a consideration of the Soviet Union's role in the region and its implications for American national security. Over the last quarter of a century, with the imposition in Cuba of a Communist regime allied with Moscow, the Soviet Union has steadily, if at times imperceptibly, expanded its power and presence in the region. This steady advance, which is reflected in Soviet doctrinal shifts registering Moscow's heightened capabilities and ambitions in the region, has been marked by an immense increase in Cuba's military capability and greatly stepped up aid to regional insurgent forces. With the coming to power in 1979 of pro-Cuban groups in Nicaragua and Grenada, the ability of the Soviet Union and Cuba to promote armed struggle and to project military power throughout the region was vastly enhanced. . . .

Cuban Strategy Revealed

The revolutionary strategy pursued by Cuba in target countries involved the creation of separate military and political fronts, as well as the establishment by such fronts of relations with a broad array of non-Communist allies, both domestic and foreign. This strategy, as it developed in the course of the Nicaraguan revolution, required in the first instance the unification of traditionally splintered insurgent groups as a condition for increased Cuban military advice and assistance. Just as the creation of such unified military fronts allowed Cuba to exercise control over the armed struggle, so too did the creation of broad political fronts with non-Communist oppositionists allow the guerrillas to coopt such forces and neutralize them as rival alternatives to the existing government. This objective was also served by the armed struggle itself, which undermined the political center by sharpening the increasingly violent confrontation between left and right.

The popular-front tactic had the added advantage of allowing the guerrillas to disarm critics by posing as non-Communist democrats, a posture given further credibility by the alliances formed with non-Communist Latin governments, European Socialists, political forces in the United States, and church and human rights groups. These alliances strengthened the international legitimacy of the guerrillas and helped delegitimize the target government, and they neutralized U.S. opposition even as they legitimized support from Cuba as just one of many foreign backers of the insurgents.

This highly sophisticated and subtle strategy was successfully applied in Nicaragua, with far-reaching consequences for the future of Central America. In March 1979, after more than a year of effort, Castro announced the unification of the three guerrilla factions of the Sandinista National Liberation Front (FSLN). During the next three months, Cuba escalated—but also cleverly masked—its military involvement, transshipping through Panama to Costa Rica 450 tons of weapons for use in the "final offensive." It also provided the FSLN with some 200 military advisers, who manned the heavy artillery and other sophisticated weapons, and with an "internationalist brigade" drawn from Central and South American terrorist groups. In addition, an intelligence center was set up at the Cuban Embassy in San Jose under the control of Julian Lopez, the DGI officer sent to Costa Rica the previous year to coordinate Cuba's assistance to the FSLN. . . .

Exporting Revolution

The effort to export the Nicaraguan revolution to El Salvador began almost as soon as the Sandinistas had seized power in Managua. As had earlier been the case in Nicaragua, the first priority was to unite the various Salvadoran guerrilla factions. A meeting in Havana in December 1979 resulted in an initial unity agreement, after which a combined military command was formed called the Unified Revolutionary Directorate (DRU). A

cc The Washington Times, 1983, reprinted with permission.

joint command and control apparatus was established in the Managua area, and logistic and training support for the guerrillas was organized on Nicaraguan soil with Cuban and other Soviet Bloc assistance.

The training of the Salvadoran guerrillas in military tactics, sabotage, explosives, and special commando operations has taken place in Cuba as well as in Nicaragua. One Salvadoran guerrilla who defected to Honduras in September 1981, for example, reported that he and 12 others were sent for training from Nicaragua to Cuba, where over 900 other Salvadorans were also being trained. . . .

El Salvador has not been the only target of the armed struggle in Central America. Guatemala exemplifies Cuban and Nicaraguan efforts to create a unified guerrilla command as a first step in mounting a sustained insurgency. In the fall of 1980 the four major Guatemalan guerrilla groups met in Managua to negotiate a unity agreement. It was signed in November—in Managua—in the presence of Manuel Pineiro Losada, the Chief of Cuba's Americas Department. Following the unity agreement, which set the goal of establishing a Marxist-Leninist state, Cuba agreed to increase military training and assistance for the Guatemalan guerrillas, including instruction in the use of heavy weapons. Arms smuggled from Nicaragua overland through Honduras have included 50mm mortars, submachine guns, rocket launchers, and M-16 rifles that have been traced to U.S. forces in Vietnam.

Guatemalan Revolution

Reflecting the Nicaraguan experience, the Guatemalan guerrillas have adopted a comprehensive political-military strategy which combines a commitment to prolonged armed struggle with an awareness of the need to establish popular front organizations and links with the media, churches of all denominations, human rights organizations, trade unions, political parties, and sympathetic governments. A General Revolutionary Command (CGR) has been established by the leaders of the four insurgent groups to plan military strategies and strengthen ties to front organizations and international solidarity networks in Mexico, Central America, the United States, and Europe.

Honduras has also become a target of Cuban and Nicaraguan assisted armed struggle. Until 1981, Havana and Managua maintained links with Honduran terrorist groups primarily for the purpose of transporting arms to insurgents in El Salvador and Guatemala. At the same time, the ground was laid for armed struggle with the formation of the Morazanist Front for the Liberation of Honduras (FMLH). In *El Nuevo Diario*, the pro-government Nicaraguan newspaper, a founder of the FMLH described it as a political-military organization formed as part of the "increasing regionalization of the Central American conflict." Evidence of Nicaraguan and Cuban involvement came when Honduran authorities raided several guerrilla safehouses in late November 1981, detaining a number of guerrillas, including several Nicaraguans. Captured documents and statements by detained guerrillas revealed that the group was formed in Nicaragua at the instigation of high-level Sandinist leaders, that its chief of operations resided in Nicaragua, and that members of the group had received military training in Nicaragua and Cuba. . . .

Cuba's Foothold

In Nicaragua, the authoritarian regime of President Somoza had become so corrupt and repressive that people were searching desperately for more freedom and a chance for greater economic opportunities. But the people of Nicaragua soon lost control of their own destinies. Castro-exported revolutionaries gained control of the supposedly home-grown Sandinista Movement. When Somoza was overthrown, rather than freedom, the people found themselves living in one of the most oppressive and militaristic socialist states in the western hemisphere. "Democracy" is a term of the past. Free elections are non-existent. Cuban "advisors" abound and Castro has a firm foothold in Central America. With support from Marxist-Leninist movements around the world, including the Soviet Union, of course, he has begun efforts to destabilize the region. He has done a good job of it.

J. Allen Cuerton, in a speech delivered in West Virginia, on February 20, 1984.

The cumulative effect of the armed assault on Central America and of the overall growth of Soviet and Cuban military power in the Caribbean Basin has been to pose a major threat to the "strategic rear" of the United States. The view that U.S. security is only threatened by the establishment of Soviet military bases in the region or by the deployment of SS-20 missiles there—a step repeatedly threatened by the Soviets, most recently by the chief of the Warsaw Pact forces in connection with the planned deployment of U.S. intermediate range missiles in Europe—overlooks the vital strategic importance to the United States of a secure Basin.

"There is no proof. . .that the rebels have received continuous and massive arms shipments from Marxist governments and that those shipments define the nature of the conflict."

Cuba Is Not Responsible for the Conflict

Phillip Berryman

Phillip Berryman is a writer who began working in Central America in 1965 researching the role of the Catholic Church in Latin America. From 1976 to 1980 while a Central American representative for the American Friends Service Committee, he was in a position to observe the deepening crisis in the region. He returned to the US from Guatemala in 1980 and has since published numerous articles in leading Christian journals and a book, *The Religious Roots of Rebellion*. In the following viewpoint, Mr. Berryman contends that US efforts to pin all revolutionary opposition in Central America to Cuban involvement is fallacious.

As you read, consider the following questions:

1. Why does the author believe that the US is mistaken when it calls revolutionary movements in Central America Marxist?
2. Does the author believe the guerrillas belong to the Communist party?
3. Is Cuba exporting arms to Central America, according to the author?

Phillip Berryman, "What's Wrong With Central America and What to Do about It," pamphlet published by The American Friends Service Committee, 1501 Cherry Street, Philadelphia, PA, 19102. Reprinted with permission.

United States policy in Central America has been based on a series of assumptions about the opposition revolutionary movements: that they are Marxist, that they would align with the Soviet Union if they took power, and that therefore American economic interests would suffer and American security would be endangered. On this point differences in U.S. public opinion have largely been over emphasis and means to be employed: conservatives speak of "dominoes" or "Soviet hit lists," while establishment liberals are more likely to worry that right wing success in the Salvadorean election results might ultimately lead to a left victory by eliminating the political "center."

These assumptions are not shared by most Western European governments nor by Mexico and several other Latin American governments. In August 1981 Mexico and France recognized El Salvador's Revolutionary Democratic Front as a "representative political force." In March 1982 Mexican president José Lopez Portillo made a serious peace proposal for the region, and later in the year Venezuela which had previously supported U.S. policy joined Mexico in urging a negotiated approach. These initiatives were rebuffed by the United States. Although these governments are quite aware of the Marxist nature of the guerrilla organizations, they evidently did not agree that U.S. policies aimed at military victory were in the real interests of the West.

Understanding the Past

In part, these countries based their positions on their understanding of the origins of the present crisis and of the process leading up to it. One notes in U.S. policy makers not only a series of factual errors, and a basic lack of understanding of previous history, but even more telling, a thorough disregard for that history. To take only one example, the February 1981 "White Paper" on El Salvador was full of chronologies but mentioned only one date prior to 1979—as though the previous history had no relevance. . . .

The crisis and repression of recent years have pushed many people into active organized opposition and this is what is essential for adequately comprehending the present situation. Establishment liberals especially tend to see the problem as one of finding the "right" group to run the government. In such a scheme elections are important for conferring legitimacy. But ordinary people are still assumed to be *clients for political leaders* rather than *protagonists in a struggle*. Policies predicated on such assumptions and categories will fail.

Today many speak of "political" solutions in Central America whether they have in mind negotiations or (controlled) elections. What is overlooked is that the *rise of the popular organizations* during the mid- to late- 1970s was a *thoroughly political process,* even though it took place largely outside the channels of existing political parties. It was precisely the violent repression of these movements which led to the state of insurrection. *Any "political" solution which ignores that earlier history is doomed to failure.*

Understanding Opposition Movements

A recognition of the importance of the "popular organizations" leads to a better understanding of the opposition movements in Guatemala and El Salvador. Conventional treatments speak of a few thousand guerrillas and occasionally add that there are a few thousand more "supporters." In El Salvador, however, the opposition speaks of various "levels" of struggle: that of the guerrilla forces themselves, that of the "militia" (people with some military training who act in an essentially defensive role at the village level), and the *organizados* ("organized," people belonging to the popular organizations). If these latter number in the hundreds of thousands, an exclusive focus on the guerrillas becomes quite misleading.

===

Cuba Not the Real Threat

Our allies in Latin America stand ready to fashion a diplomatic solution to the Central American crisis but not to lend their good offices to the principle that all nations are sovereign but some more sovereign than others.

So the choice. . .narrows to getting peace or getting its way. Peace can be had, should Washington throw its weight behind Contadora's 21 points. It is a peace, moreover, that should satisfy both the true interests of the U.S. and U.S. politicians' fear of public backlash. Why? Because Contadora effectively rules out a significant Soviet or Cuban military presence in Central America.

The price Washington must pay for that peaceful resolution is toleration of revolutionary movements *inside* the borders of Central American nations. In exchange for peace, Washington must give up control—control over things it has no right to manage, even if its intentions were the best in the world, which they're not.

Eldon Kenworthy, *In These Times*, March 21-27, 1984.

===

It is to the guerrilla (or, as they prefer, "politico-military") organizations that we now turn to consider their origins and development, their ideologies, and their outside connections.

The Guatemalan guerrilla struggle began in a barracks revolt in the army in 1960 and became a serious guerrilla movement in the middle of that decade until it was almost wiped out (with thousands of peasants killed) around 1970. Today the four main groups, EGP, ORPA, FAR, and PGT, all trace their origins to that earlier struggle. Nicaragua's Sandinista National Liberation Front was formed in 1961 and was almost wiped out several times, remaining relatively small until 1978. Two Salvadorean groups, the FPL and ERP were formed around 1970; a split in ERP later led to the formation of the FARN.

It is quite important to notice that in all these countries the main guerrilla organizations, despite their Marxist ideology, arose independently of the existing Communist Party or even as alternatives to it. . . . Central American Communist parties, all of which were small, followed the overall line from Moscow, which after a brief dalliance with guerrilla struggle in the early 1960s, called for legal activity. Thus into the very late 1970s the Communist parties of these countries were cautious, e.g., the Salvadorean Communist Party did not fully endorse armed struggle until May 1980.

Communist Parties Involvement

This fact should be appreciated from the viewpoint of the other revolutionary organizations. While they were risking their lives both in armed struggle and in the accompanying clandestine political work, the Communist parties were limiting themselves to legal activities and denouncing guerrilla struggle as adventurism. In all three countries the Communist parties are the smallest, least successful, and least respected components of the guerrilla coalitions. While they might be welcomed into an alliance, they will be in no position to exercise a dominant influence.

Ideologically, the guerrilla organizations have not followed any international "line." Despite occasional suggestions that one or another group in El Salvador is "Maoist" or "Trotskyite" all evidence indicates that the splits among the organizations reflect different origins and different concepts of strategy. The Sandinistas were divided between those who favored a "prolonged peoples' war," largely peasant based; those who argued for working with the "proletariat"; and those who judged it feasible to work for a rapid popular uprising. The organizations in El Salvador were divided along similar lines. In Guatemala there seems to have been less disagreement on fundamental strategy, but organizations have operated in different regions and used different methods.

Marxist Nature Mixed

The Marxism of these groups shows little theoretical precision; rather than study Marx they have studied their countries, using

Marxist concepts, e.g., Jaime Wheelock, today a top Sandinista commander, wrote a book analyzing the dominant economic groups in Nicaragua. Ideologically, their Marxism is largely "home grown." In Guatemala, the revolutionary organizations have had to deal with the "Indian question," one on which Marxist theory has little to say. In all three countries the presence of Christians has had an important influence, tempering some tendencies of Marxist ideology. ORPA, the second most important guerrilla group in Guatemala, claims it is not Marxist.

Myth: Cubans Are Everywhere

According to this myth, Cuban agents are fomenting revolution all over the world. Anywhere the interests of the United States or its allies are in trouble, the Cubans are there. During the 1960s, there were almost daily reports of Cuba's subversive activities in Argentina, student strikes in Colombia, nationalist riots in Panama, drug trafficking in Puerto Rico, and a civil war in the Dominican Republic. The Cubans were even said to have trained the Black Panthers.

With time, each of these charges has been proved either vastly exaggerated or completely untrue. Although Castro's revolution did inspire many Latin American radicals of the 1960s, Cuba's actual matériel and personnel commitments to the region were comparatively small. Throughout the 1960s, there were never more than a few hundred Cubans fighting in all of Latin America.

Carla Anne Robbins, *The Cuban Threat*, 1983.

Throughout most of their existence the guerrilla groups were small in number and carried out only occasional actions. In late 1977 the Sandinistas began to move into the offensive. Similarly in Guatemala guerrilla groups stepped up their actions in 1979. Surprisingly, it was as late as 1980 that Salvadorean guerrilla organizations became engaged in major military actions. In all three cases there was a common pattern of arriving at unity among the various guerrilla organizations or factions, and then among organizations representing vast sectors of society (labor, peasants, slumdwellers, professionals, political parties and Church groups).

Even though guerrilla organizations arose independently of, and in some cases in opposition to, Communist parties, they have maintained relations with Cuba. Their cadres took refuge there when they had to flee their own country and some received training. Ché Guevara appears on the logo of Guatemala's EGP. It seems clear, however, that neither Cuba nor the Soviet Union saw any chance for revolutionary success in Central

116

America until the Sandinistas were close to victory. The Soviet leadership does not seem to have expected to gain allies in its adversary's "backyard." Late in the anti-Somoza struggle there was some Cuban involvement in arms delivery, but in no sense did Cuba play a determining role.

Since early 1981, however, the Reagan Administration has insisted that the Salvadorean insurgents have been receiving substantial arms and ammunition shipments from Nicaragua (and therefore from Cuba, backed by the Soviet Union). It has frequently spoken of Guatemala's insurgency as "Cuban-backed" and has spoken of Central America offering a "textbook case" of communist interference.

Communist Expansionism?

The point is important because it has become the Reagan Administration's definition of the problem: all previous history, well-documented massive atrocities, the objections of other nations—all are shoved aside as irrelevant in the face of "communist expansionism." (U.S. policy makers have shown a similar pattern of blocking out the particularities of nations and peoples with their own histories and struggles in regard to Indochina a few years ago and the Middle East to this day.)

What must be emphasized is quite simple: *at no point has the Administration furnished credible proof for its accusations.* It has sometimes stated that it has such proof but the public is essentially expected to accept the accusations on faith.

The February 1981 "White Paper" on El Salvador was found to be full of mistaken identities and unjustified extrapolations, as reported in the Washington *Post* and the *Wall St. Journal*, e.g., the documents offered no proof for the assertion that 200 tons of weapons had gone from Nicaragua to El Salvador. There were reasons for suspecting that some of the documents were fabricated.

Despite the Administration's claims and millions of dollars of military aid given to Honduras, ostensibly to stop such an arms flow, there has been no interception of a major arms shipment from Nicaragua. A tractor trailer with M-16s, stopped in January 1981, had started from Costa Rica. Some attempts to prove Nicaraguan involvement in arms shipping have proved to be untrue (e.g., an alleged landing from boats in January 1981) and others embarrassing (the young Nicaraguan brought from El Salvador by the State Department as proof of Sandinista involvement, who instead told a press conference he had gone to El Salvador on his own and had been tortured by the Salvadorean military).

Another reason for skepticism is the fact that reporters and film crews in rebel-held territory have found a heterogeneous assortment of weapons rather than the uniform equipment one would expect if there were systematic shipments.

Origins of Arms Shipments

Where have the insurgents obtained their arms? They claim they have acquired them from a variety of sources: the international arms markets, including dealers in the United States, and the Salvadorean military itself, either by capturing weapons or buying them from opportunistic officers.

The point being made here is essentially negative, namely that there is no proof for the Administration's assertion that the rebels have received continuous and massive arms shipments from Marxist governments and that those shipments define the nature of the conflict.

On the contrary: the struggle in Central America has emerged not only from people's poverty but from declining real living standards, due especially to rural landlessness; as existing forms of action (elections) proved impotent, people formed new militant organizations, and as these were met with violence they became more united and eventually joined with guerrilla organizations which, while they are largely Marxist, are genuinely Central American and are not dependent on the Soviet Union.

"Every day dozens of Central Americans. . .are sacrificed to [the] quest for U.S. credibility."

US Search for Credibility Is Promoting the Conflict

Eldon Kenworthy

Eldon Kenworthy is an associate professor of government at Cornell University. He is a Latin American Specialist. In the following viewpoint, Mr. Kenworthy argues that US attempts to prove its resolve and credibility in Central America have intensified the conflict and limited diplomatic choices.

As you read, consider the following questions:

1. Why in the author's opinion is US credibility in question in Central America?
2. Why does the author believe that the crisis in Central America for the US "is in no small part its own creation"?
3. How does a preoccupation with a global image affect the US, according to the author?

Eldon Kenworthy, "Why the U.S. is in Central America," *Bulletin of the Atomic Scientists,* October 1983. Reprinted by permission of THE BULLETIN OF THE ATOMIC SCIENTISTS, a magazine of science and public affairs. Copyright 1983 by the Educational Foundation for Nuclear Science, Chicago, IL 60637.

What explains the Administration's persistence in casting the Central American crisis in simplistic East-West terms, despite the critical feedback this elicits and despite the tendency of this formulation to escalate the stakes while closing off options?

The tack taken by the Reagan Administration can be traced back to position papers written during the 1980 presidential campaign. The Committee of Santa Fe's "A New Inter-American Policy for the Eighties," for example, proclaimed that World War III was underway and that Latin America was one of its principal theaters: "In war there is no substitute for victory."

What attracted candidate Reagan to Jeane Kirkpatrick was not her understanding of Central America. She is, in fact, miscast as a Latin American expert. Before being named Chief U.S. Delegate to the United Nations she apparently had neither visited the region nor studied it in depth. Her earlier book on Peronism was based on data collected by an Argentine polling organization hired for that purpose. What attracted Reagan was Kirkpatrick's ability to subsume Third World conflicts under Cold War categories. In the *Commentary* article that caught Reagan's eye, she reduced such struggle to friendly autocrats (potential democrats) challenged by Soviet-manipulated guerrillas. The primary concern of U.S. policy, Kirkpatrick argued, is to maintain credibility. Otherwise "our friends" will think "the U.S. cannot be counted on in times of difficulty and our enemies will have observed that American support provides no security against the forward march of history." Reagan's first Secretary of State, Alexander Haig, saw Central America as a relatively safe arena for demonstrating to the world that the United States had recovered from Vietnam: "I know the American people will support what is prudent and necessary providing they think we mean what we mean and that we are going to succeed and not flounder as we did in Vietnam.". . .

This leaves unanalyzed, however, the *content* of that rigid approach—the credibility to which Kirkpatrick refers. This theme, to which the President repeatedly returns, is clearly seen in his address to a joint session of Congress, called to rally support for more military aid to El Salvador.

> If Central America were to fall, what would the consequences be for our position in Asia and Europe and for alliances such as NATO? If the United States cannot respond to a threat near our own borders, why should Europeans or Asians believe we are seriously concerned about threats to them?

And at the close of this speech:

> The national security of all the Americas is at stake in Central America. If we cannot defend ourselves there, we cannot expect to prevail elsewhere. Our credibility would collapse, our alliances would crumble.

Reagan continues to reiterate this point. In May he told the Cuban community in Miami that "If we cannot act decisively so close to home, who will believe us anywhere?" At a press conference in July, the President was asked if his Administration's stated opposition to the use of force in Central America might be contradicted by the unilateral dispatch of nearly a quarter of available U.S. naval power to that region. He replied that reducing our military presence would be "the wrong kind of signal to send" the Soviets and the Cubans, who are the source of "the trouble that is going on down there."

Dominant Theme of Credibility

A dominant theme in U.S. policy toward Central America, then, is credibility—a term closely associated with Henry Kissinger, appointed by President Reagan to head a Bipartisan Commission on Central America. "If we cannot manage Central America," according to Kissinger, "it will be impossible to convince threatened nations in the Persian Gulf and in other places that we know how to manage the global equilibrium." What is credibility? And why is U.S. credibility at stake in a region of small, underdeveloped nations that lie in our shadow?

U.S. credibility is in question in Central America for the simple reason that superpowers are assumed to be capable of getting

Ben Sargent *The Austin American Statesman*, reprinted with permission.

what they want within their own spheres of influence, if not by persuasion then by force. As exceptions, Yugoslavia and Cuba only strengthened the rule. The Johnson-Brezhnev doctrine of the mid-1960s represented a tacit agreement between the two superpowers not to press an advantage inside the other's sphere of influence, out of mutual recognition that "another Cuba" or "another Yugoslavia" was unacceptable to either power. In Poland and Nicaragua today one sees each superpower testing the limits of this agreement while remaining careful not to cross a threshold of direct political-military intervention.

While offering aid and a lot of "fraternal sympathy" to the "heroic revolutionaries" of Central America, Soviet leaders stop short of promising to come to their rescue, militarily or economically. Washington has adopted a similar posture with regard to Poland. Cuba is different for the Soviets, as West Berlin is for the United States. These affiliations resulted from superpower confrontations of a previous period. The high risks these showdowns entailed motivated the Johnson-Brezhnev understanding.

It is possible, of course, for both superpowers to observe the limits established by 1965 and still suffer a defection. Nicaragua is one such case, Poland a potential second. In short, through largely internal causes and without decisive intervention from abroad, a client country may reject its patron. The humiliation to the rejected superpower is no less great than it would be had the opposing superpower engineered the defection. Indeed, it may be worse, since the repudiation was chosen by the satellite rather than foisted upon it.

Caring About Public Opinion

It is at this point that we confront an important truth about credibility. To Washington it may not matter what the Soviet role was or is in Central America. It may not matter that the Nicaraguans, for reasons readily apparent to anyone who examines their history, freely support a revolution that repudiates U.S. imperialism and Central American-style capitalism. What matters to President Reagan and his advisors is that this defection is likely to be *viewed* at home and abroad as a loss for the United States and a gain for "world communism." In an important sense, Soviet and Nicaraguan behavior is not at issue. What matters is the *perception* others—voters here and leaders in Riyadh, Ankara, Bonn and Buenos Aires—may get of U.S. "resolve" or "will."

"Events that used to be local," Henry Kissinger wrote in *The White House Years*, "assume global significance." The operative word is "significance," which is what onlookers bring to an event, not something inherent in it. Thus it matters less whether "world communism" actually exists as an entity than that U.S. credibility is tied to people thinking this could be the case—matters, that is, to President Reagan and his advisors.

For a superpower not to intervene to obtain at least the appearance of success within its own sphere of influence is thought to indicate incompetence or loss of nerve. Allies and enemies in distant lands will think us weak if, having the means, we do not impose our purposes on Central America. Or so it is believed.

US Sphere of Influence

At first blush, it is hard to conceive of any Central American nation presenting a test of U.S. credibility. The gross national product of any of these countries is a poor match for the annual sales of one of our supermarket chains. In territory, Oregon is larger than Nicaragua, El Salvador, and Guatemala combined. Central America's natural resources are few and redundant, its populations poor and its markets small. U.S. credibility is implicated in Central America not because of what these countries are but presumably because of where they are located. Central America lies inside our sphere of influence. For a superpower not to intervene to obtain at least the appearance of success within its own sphere of influence is thought to communicate incompetence of loss of nerve. Allies and enemies in distant lands will think us weak if we do not impose our will. It is precisely within a big power's sphere of influence that it is assumed to always have the means.

Eldon Kenworthy, *World Policy*, Fall '83.

At issue, then, is less what is actually happening in Central America than how those happenings are perceived by leaders and publics that "truly" account. The National Security Council's leaked document, "U.S. Policy in Central America and Cuba Through Fiscal Year 1984," reveals disdain for the Mexican government's reactions, since this "domino" has the temerity not to see itself as such. Washington maintains credibility when relevant others think it means business. Since Washington anticipates how these audiences will react, the correct formula for credibility becomes: We have it when we think they think we mean business. . . .

No doubt the Administration would like to see American credibility restored without resorting to direct military intervention. If the possibilities for restoring credibility by other means dwindle, however, the choice will come down to using military force or losing credibility. When a U.S. President speaks of "the first real Communist aggression on the American mainland," as Reagan did to the longshoremen in July, one hears echoes of

John Foster Dulles in 1954 and of Lyndon Johnson in 1964. Whenever a Central American-Caribbean situation has been defined in those terms, Washington has used military action to get what it wants.

This Administration's preoccupation with credibility is linked to behavior that critics, even friends, of the Reagan Administration find confusing and counterproductive: missed diplomatic opportunities, soured hemispheric relations, military risks. The crisis the Administration now faces is in no small part its own creation. In Central America, unlike Indochina, the United States did not (and still does not) confront the vital interests of a rival power. Given the realities of geography and underdevelopment, Washington might have remained as influential in Central America as the Soviets remained peripheral, if only the White House had played its cards calmly.

Persuading the People

Herein lies one of the ironies of a foreign policy wedded to perception. To show "resolve" in Central America, Congress and the U.S. public must be persuaded that the stakes are high; that, in the President's words, "we have a vital interest, a moral duty and a solemn responsibility" comparable to those confronting the Truman Administration in the early months of the Cold War. Only if such persuasion succeeds will funds be forthcoming for that demonstration of U.S. power on which credibility depends. Yet, by making the case to Congress and the public in this overblown way, the Administration escalates the test it then must meet to salvage credibility. . . .

Among those most influential in shaping U.S. policy toward Central America today, the approach criticized here is considered hard-headed realism. I have tried to show how preoccupation with a U.S. global image directs attention away from the reality at hand; how it fosters an infantile approach to complex situations; and how it costs Washington diplomatic options. Like Narcissus, the White House scans the surface of Central America for its own reflection, its gaze rarely penetrating that surface to discover a reality quite different from its own.

People Sacrificed to Credibility

Every day dozens of Central Americans—mothers, children, peasants, youths, many just trying to mind their own business—are sacrificed to this quest for U.S. credibility. I know no other way to describe a situation in which Washington introduces attack jets and strafing helicopters into densely populated countrysides, knowing as little as it does of the actual situation in those areas. As it "stays the course" in Central America, this Administration increases the likelihood that those daily sacrifices will include North Americans as well.

"By pouring money into the Nicaraguan economy and Somoza's National Guard, Kennedy, Johnson, and Nixon inadvertently helped create the conditions for the revolution."

US Economic Aid Is Promoting the Conflict

Walter LaFeber

Walter LaFeber is the Marie Underhill Noll Professor of American History at Cornell University. A distinguished educator, he is also the author of numerous books including *America in the Cold War* and *The Panama Canal: The Crisis in Historical Perspective*. His recent work, *Inevitable Revolutions: The United States in Central America*, deals with US and Central American relations. In the following viewpoint, Mr. LaFeber illustrates why he believes that massive US economic aid has increased the gap between the rich and the poor in Central America thereby contributing to revolutionary activity.

As you read, consider the following questions:

1. Does the author believe that President Kennedy's "Alliance for Progress" worked in Central America?
2. How did US policy in Nicaragua undermine that country's stability, according to the author?
3. Does the author think Central American revolution can be prevented? Why or why not?

Walter LaFeber, "Inevitable Revolutions," *The Atlantic Monthly*, June 1982. Reprinted with permission of the author.

When President John F. Kennedy announced the Alliance for Progress in March of 1961, he proclaimed, "Let us again transform the [Western Hemisphere] into a vast crucible of revolutionary ideas and efforts.". . .

Twenty years after Kennedy initiated the Alliance, revolutionary ideas and efforts are tearing Central America apart. Having learned few lessons from the past, Ronald Reagan is responding with large economic-aid programs ($350 million for the embattled Caribbean Basin countries alone) and counterinsurgency-warfare training. After two decades of policies that contributed to the spread of both poverty and left-wing revolutions, Reagan is attempting to destroy those revolutions by repeating the policies.

Owing in part to its ignorance of history, the Reagan Administration has refused to question a fundamental assumption that shaped Kennedy's foreign policy: the larger a nation's economy grows, the happier that nation has to be. Nowhere has this assumption been proved more false than in Central America. Of the five nations in the area—Nicaragua, Guatemala, El Salvador, Honduras, and Costa Rica—three seemed to prosper during the 1960s. Nicaragua's annual per capita growth rate rose 5.3 percent, Guatemala's rose 3 percent, and El Salvador's rose 2.8 percent despite an extraordinarily high birthrate. Within ten years after Alliance officials acclaimed those figures, revolutionaries had overthrown the Nicaraguan government and besieged El Salvador's. Guatemala's military regime saved itself, at least temporarily, by murdering and torturing opponents in large numbers. The only Central American country that remained both democratic and free of leftist disturbances during the 1960s and 1970s was Costa Rica. In the 1960s, that nation also had the lowest annual growth rate (.8 percent) in the region. . . .

The most important conclusion to be drawn from the Central American growth figures is, therefore, that the Alliance could help only those government officials who helped their people and not merely themselves. . . .

US Policies Worsened Situation

By the time of Kennedy's death, in November of 1963, Alliance policies had apparently worsened the economic situation they aimed to improve. The plan was victimized by bureaucratic jealousies in Washington and by conservatives' foot-dragging in Latin America. Most important, the Alliance rested on the false belief that growth produced by New Deal-style development programs could work in El Salvador, where the fabled "Fourteen Families" held tight to every vestige of their immense economic and political power; in Nicaragua, where the Somoza family multiplied its wealth; and in Guatemala, where ruling military officers fought each other for larger shares of the country's resources. . . .

Military Assistance Grew

As economic hopes for the Alliance dwindled, the military component grew. As reform efforts failed, the need for armed force increased. In retrospect, this changing balance between the economic and military parts of the Alliance was an admission of the plan's failure to touch the root causes of the national revolutions. Economic and military policies had actually been closely linked from the start. Attorney General Robert Kennedy had passed Federal Bureau of Investigation reports to his brother warning that security in Central America was "extremely deficient." Military assistance flowed into the area in ever larger amounts. Between 1950 and 1963, for example, Guatemala received only $5.3 million in military aid; but the amount doubled to $10.9 million between the years 1964 and 1967. For Nicaragua, the comparable figures were $4.5 million during the first thirteen years and $7.5 million in the next three. . . .

Economic Aid Siphoned Off

Here in Latin America, a large part of what gets in through the front door goes out through the back. The flight of capital drained more than half of the foreign credits obtained by Mexico and Venezuela in the last three years, and one-third or those obtained by Argentina. In the same period, some $15 billion was invested in real estate or deposited in foreign banks by Central Americans. This is nearly twice the sum that the Kissinger commission proposed for the region—$8 billion in five years. . . .

Assistance programs are clearly not the key. Political reform is urgent and indispensable. Without it, nothing will help. Before anything else, something must be done about the political ignominy that has produced the meadow that ignites with just one spark.

Luís Burstin, *The New York Times*, February 9, 1984.

No one in Washington could come up with a better, or easier, solution than turning to the military. In 1964, the CIA warned Johnson that the Alliance was creating unstable conditions. The growing demand in Latin America for "positive and radical changes in the inequitable and backward socio-economic structures and for gains in levels of living are mounting steadily," the Agency reported. Worse, an alternative model was at hand: "Cuba's experiment with almost total state socialism is being watched closely by other nations in the hemisphere." The CIA added that "any appearance of success there [Cuba] could have an extensive impact on the statist trend elsewhere in the area." With the Alliance malfunctioning, a memorandum from the State Department, not the Pentagon, drew the lesson for Johnson: "The pace of social upheaval is likely to increase in the next ten years," so the administration must maintain "predominant United States military influence" in Latin America and place "continued emphasis" on "internal security programs.". . .

By the late 1960s, the Alliance had become a highly volatile mixture. It emphasized private investment that worked with wealthy elites and worsened an already glaring economic imbalance. Protected by Washington's embrace, these elites refused to offer socio-political change even as Central American revolutionary forces grew in number; they relied instead on U.S.-trained and -supplied military forces to maintain order through repression. North American promises of development had raised but could never meet Central American hopes. No wonder that the three nations in the area that had supposedly benefited most from the Alliance, economically and militarily—Nicaragua, El Salvador, and Guatemala—were beset by growing opposition movements. . . .

Policies in Nicaragua

In Nicaragua, the Alliance. . .operated in a country that seemed to be as stable as any in Latin America. U.S. policy, however, helped undermine that stability. Dollars flowed into agricultural projects that enriched the 2 percent of the farms, the great *latifundios*, that occupied nearly half the nation's usable land. The Somoza family alone owned territory nearly the size of El Salvador. As these giant farms expanded their cotton and other export crops, they forced peasants off the land and into towns, where jobs were scarce. Some of the displaced returned to their fields and squatted illegally so they could grow food for their families' survival. After a half-dozen years of the Alliance, only 50 percent of the population—and 2 percent of those living in rural areas—had access to potable water. Despite U.S. health programs, the major causes of death continued to be gastrointestinal and parasitic diseases and infant disorders. . . .

During the years of the Alliance an even more dangerous opponent for Somoza began to emerge. In 1961, a new guerrilla organization, the Sandinista National Liberation Front (FSLN), was founded by Nicaraguans in Havana. Named after Somoza's victim of 1934, the Sandinistas posed little threat to the Somoza regime until 1966, when they began urban terrorist campaigns. The Johnson Administration responded automatically. Within a

COVERT U.S. AID   OVERT U.S. AID

Marlette, *The Charlotte Observer*, reprinted with permission.

year, twenty-five U.S. military advisers resided in Nicaragua, and the Pentagon increased military assistance. The FSLN nevertheless grew, as the landless labor force in some areas was more than ten times as large in the 1970s as it had been before the Alliance began. . . .

The Nicaraguans did not forget that the United States had supported Somoza to the end. Nor could they ignore the way North American economic policies had been used to help overthrow Latin American governments in the past, particularly Salvador Allende's elected government in Chile in 1973. They were as suspicious of U.S. intentions as Washington was of their request to Cuba for technicians who could quickly construct educational and health facilities. Walter Duncan, vice president of the American Chamber of Commerce in Latin America and owner of an industrial chemical firm in Managua, told a Senate committee in 1979 that multilateral aid, not direct U.S. assistance, could be most useful: "We [North Americans] are suspect any time we help any of these people. They are paranoid.". . .

By pouring money into the Nicaraguan economy and Somoza's National Guard, Kennedy, Johnson, and Nixon inadvertently helped create the conditions for the revolution that seized power in 1979. Carter's policies and the Sandinistas' quest for self-sufficiency intensified the mutual suspicion. Reagan's withdrawal of support and Haig's threats only drove the revolution further to the left. U.S. policy-makers seem to have tried for twenty years to bring about the kind of revolution that the

Alliance for Progress was supposed to prevent. . . .

The same conclusion could be drawn about U.S. policy toward the nation that was next threatened by revolution. El Salvador received more Alliance funds than any other Central American country. Between 1962 and 1966 alone, $63 million of U.S. government monies were given to the ruling oligarchs to invest, and private investments increased until the U.S. was a dominant influence in the transportation, oil-refining, and electric-power sectors. In 1964-1965, the economic growth rate reached an extraordinary 12 percent. Hundreds of new industries appeared, and the country soon possessed the largest number of manufacturing plants in Central America. An annual $1 million of U.S. military assistance gave the small but tightly knit army the weapons and training it needed. El Salvador, the Johnson Administration announced, was "a model for the other Alliance countries.". . .

The oligarchs passed the reform laws demanded by Kennedy and then made sure that the laws were not put into effect. The ruling families channeled Alliance aid into their own industrial enterprises or used it to buy up more land, on which they grew crops for export rather than food for their countrymen. As Alliance funds helped sugar exports rise more than 1,000 percent between 1960 and 1970, thousands of Salvadorans were evicted from land so that more sugar could be grown. Throughout this century, the amount of land under cultivation has increased as growing numbers of Salvadorans have starved. By the late 1960s, the country was exporting huge amounts of coffee, cotton, and sugar, but the general population ranked among the five worst-nourished peoples in the world. El Salvador nevertheless remained stable. In 1967, a U.S. Senate-sponsored analysis gave the reason: this model of the Alliance was found to be among the hemisphere's most militaristic regimes, so it had not been troubled by the "popular revolutionary stirrings" that afflicted other Latin American countries. . . .

Leftist Revolution

U.S. policy helped drive the revolution to the left. By defining the conflict in military terms, Washington officials forced both Ungo and Duarte to become more dependent upon their hard-line army commanders. The State Department refused to negotiate seriously with leftist moderates such as Ungo. Such negotiations could have been useful, however, only if the United States had been willing to press for discussions between the military and the left. Neither Carter nor Reagan was willing to do so. Nor would the Salvadoran officers automatically have followed Washington's advice; the last group to do that had been Somoza's National Guard, and the Salvadorans were not about to follow it into oblivion. Carter did cut off aid to the Salvadoran government in 1980, as its violations of human rights continued (including the murder of three North American nuns and a lay missionary), but he reopened the pipeline in early 1981, when the regime had to fight off a major left-wing offensive. About 30,000 people died during 1980-1981, and, according to independent groups in the best position to judge, as many as 75 percent of them were civilian victims of either government forces or vigilante groups paid by oligarchs. The massacres increased when Duarte began to redistribute land. Figures compiled by the Church showed that the largest numbers of peasants were killed in the areas where they were to receive land from the reforms. By 1982, the agrarian program had come to a stop.

Economic Aid Counterproductive

President Reagan is asking American taxpayers to give $8.4 billion for economic assistance to Central America over the next five years. It would be a waste of immense sums. Ironically, it would also strengthen precisely the forces that the President wants to destroy. . . .

Since 1981, aid to these nations has multiplied several times. The result: 10,000 Salvadoran revolutionaries now control large parts of the country; the Guatemalan economy has declined and the country has endured two military coups; Honduras is suffering its gravest economic crisis in 50 years; and the defeated contras now admit that they have no hope for establishing a government.

The Reagan response is to multiply the aid program again. The administration resembles the shirt salesman who loses $10 on each item he sells but is confident he can avoid ruin by doubling his sales.

Walter LaFeber, *San Diego Union*, March 4, 1984.

Reagan tried to deal with the spreading revolution by returning to two components of the Alliance for Progress. He doubled economic aid in 1981, to $126.5 million, and planned to double it again this year. Last February, he announced that government aid would be abetted by a Caribbean Basin program that would encourage private investment and increased trade. Reagan also revived another major component of the Alliance—military training: fifty-four U.S. advisers went to El Salvador, 500 Salvadoran officers came to the United States for training, and military aid multiplied by a factor of eight during 1981, to $40 million. The only component missing from the old Alliance program was Kennedy's request for reforms. Reagan refused to insist on effective land redistribution or an end to the massacres as a condition for aid. "Power is not negotiable," a former Salvadoran military leader announced in April of 1981. That remark meant, among other things, that elections were unacceptable unless they confirmed the power of the army. It also meant that the revolution could end only in total military victory for either one side or the other. The Reagan Administration policy depended entirely on the hope that the government would win that victory. . . .

Revolution in Guatemala

In Guatemala, the contradictions of the Alliance became visible earlier than they had in the other two countries, but Washington's policies never wavered. The result was predictable. In 1967, after six years and nearly $50 million of Alliance help (plus another $50 million of private U.S. investment during the 1960s), Guatemala ranked first on the State Department's list of Latin American nations threatened by insurgents. . . .

The revolt against the right-wing military began not among the poor but within the military itself. In late 1960, no less than one third of the army rebelled against its senior commanders. . . . The most radical looked to Castro as a model. The other chose to work with Guatemala's small, inept Communist Party. Neither group should have received much popular support, but a combination of inefficient Guatemalan governments and Alliance policies quickly propelled the insurgents to the top of the State Department's Most Dangerous list.

Despite more than $100 million in U.S. government and private investment during the 1960s, the Alliance was unable to pry any agrarian reforms out of the regime for the 80 percent of some 5 million Guatemalans who depended on the land. Nine out of ten rural families endured existences that were described in 1962 by a U.S. agricultural economist as lives "of poverty, malnutrition, sickness, superstition, and illiteracy." About 68,000 rural families survived as tenants or low-wage laborers without any land of their own, while half the country's farm area—the best half—was owned by 1,100 families. That elite group used Alliance funds to expand production of export crops, especially sugar. Meanwhile, food shortages threatened starvation in some areas, and the regime finally had to pay premium prices to import corn, beans, and rice from the United States and Colombia. . . .

The Indians, driven by poverty and encouraged by the priests, have changed the course of Guatemalan politics. The revolution is no longer conducted by elite army members, as it was in the 1960s. Nor, in 1982, do its main groups look to Havana for aid, as the leading rebel organization did fifteen years ago, although they are willing to accept aid from Cubans or from any other source. The military government and the six disparate groups that form the revolutionaries are locked in a war to the death. Atrocities are committed by both sides, but the government's actions have been so horrible that the Reagan Administration has not been able to explain away human-rights violations and resume regular arms shipments. Last year, however, the President began sending military trucks, jeeps, and helicopters, after disingeniously removing them from a list of items that the State Department can clear for shipment only after human rights have been taken into account. These supplies will hardly suffice. The revolutionary armies already have upward of 6,000 soldiers, and they grow as the economy is devastated by war. Senior Guatemalan army officers believe the government needs, instead of its present 22,000-man force, 100,000 soldiers, fully supplied with modern counterinsurgency equipment. Such assistance can come only from the United States.

Silencing the Guns

It is a fact of economic life that no aid program, regardless of how well financed or organized, will produce significant progress in an atmosphere of armed conflict. Peace must be our first priority in Central America. We must quiet the guns before we send the butter.

Christopher J. Dodd, *The San Diego Union,* March 28, 1984.

If the experiences in Nicaragua and El Salvador are guides, the U.S. will send increasing amounts of that assistance to Guatemala. And, as a predictable consequence of U.S. policy, aid designed to rescue the economy will benefit the relatively few wealthy Guatemalans and their military allies, while military assistance will be used for the killing and torturing of the poor and middle-class who join the revolution. Regardless of how high the growth rates and military-aid figures soared in Central America during the 1960s and 1970s, the attractiveness of revolution grew, in part because U.S. aid was used in ways that only widened the socio-economic differences between rich and poor. Unless fundamental structural change occurs in many so-called Caribbean Basin countries, and especially in Guatemala and El Salvador, President Reagan's Caribbean plan will, like the Alliance for Progress, only lead to intensification of the revolutions that it would like to destroy.

Revolutions in the three Central American countries can no longer be prevented. If they are to be contained, the reprieve will be only temporary unless their causes—the gross inequities that have long been accepted as natural in these societies—are removed. The United States cannot single-handedly perform that miracle, or at least not unless North Americans are willing to rule the three nations as the Soviet Union is attempting to rule Afghanistan. Throughout this century, Washington officials have proved to be poor colonial governors.

The United States would be wise to step aside and allow the revolutions to work themselves out, with the single proviso that no Soviet-controlled bases or military personnel be allowed in Central America. Washington can also use its power to promote negotiated settlements when circumstances allow, and then offer generous economic help to any regime that wants such aid and is willing to use it to improve the lives of all its people. . . .

Attempts to Stop the Tide

Since the era of Theodore Roosevelt, the United States has tried to stop Latin American revolutions. When it acted energetically, as in Cuba and Central America, the United States did little to remove the causes of unrest and, instead, frequently caused the revolutions to turn more sharply to the left. When the U.S. was unable to act energetically because of distractions (for example, World War I and the Great Depression prevented North American Presidents from cracking down on the leaders of the Mexican Revolution as they wanted to), the revolution moderated and North Americans adjusted gradually and profitably. Even with its power the United States cannot roll back the Central American revolutions. With luck, and an understanding of the past, it can, however, help bring order out of those revolutions.

Recognizing Ethnocentrism

Ethnocentrism is the attitude or tendency of people to view their race, religion, culture, group, or nation as superior to others, and to judge others on that basis. An American, whose custom is to eat with a fork or spoon, would be making an ethnocentric statement when saying, "The Chinese custom of eating with chopsticks is stupid."

Ethnocentrism has promoted much misunderstanding and conflict. It emphasizes cultural and religious differences and the notion that one's national institutions or group's customs are superior.

Ethnocentrism limits people's ability to be objective and to learn from others. Education in the truest sense stresses the similarities of the human condition throughout the world and the basic equality and dignity of all people.

Most of the following statements are taken from the viewpoints in this book. Some have other origins. Consider each statement carefully. *Mark E for any statement you think is ethnocentric. Mark N for any statement you think is not ethnocentric. Mark U if you are undecided about any statement.*

If you are doing this activity as the member of a class or group, compare your answers with those of other class or group members. Be able to defend your answers. You may discover that others will come to different conclusions than you. Listening to the reasons others present for their answers may give you valuable insights in recognizing ethnocentric statements.

If you are reading this book alone, ask others if they agree with your answers. You too will find this interaction very valuable.

> *E* = *ethnocentric*
> *N* = *not ethnocentric*
> *U* = *undecided*

1. All patriotic Americans should support US involvement in El Salvador.

2. America is a source of hope and a force for progress in Central America.

3. Two centuries ago, our nation raised the light of liberty before the world—and all of this hemisphere looked to us as an example and an inspiration.

4. It is the unethical and opportunistic government of Cuba, not the United States, that is using the tactics of insurgency to overthrow the legitimate government of El Salvador.

5. Americans should realize that the people of El Salvador are easily manipulated into joining communism.

6. In Central America, the main guerrilla organizations, despite their Marxist ideology, arose independently of the existing Communist Party.

7. The United States must prohibit the people of Central America from becoming victims of evil communist expansionists.

8. Only a democratic government protects the rights of its people.

9. There is no proof for the assertion that rebels have received continuous and massive arms shipments from Marxist governments.

10. One reason for Kennedy's Alliance for Progress was to give Central American countries economic aid.

11. Failure in Central America would be a failure for the national will of the United States.

12. The United States has a vital interest, a moral duty, and a solemn responsibility to intervene in Central America.

13. For years, the United States supported the dictatorship of Somoza in Nicaragua.

14. The Soviet Union would like to see revolution continue in Central America.

Periodical Bibliography

The following list of periodical articles deals with the subject matter of this chapter.

Elliot Abrams — "The Cuban Revolution and Its Impact on Human Rights," *Department of State Bulletin*, December 1983.

T.D. Allman — "Rising to Rebellion," *Harper's*, March 1981.

Luis Burstin — "My Talks with the Cubans," *The New Republic*, February 13, 1984.

Robert A. Dahl — "The Democracy Mystique," *The New Republic*, April 2, 1984.

Kenneth Dam — "The Caribbean Basin Initiative and Central America," *Department of State Bulletin*, January 1984.

Michael J. Englebert — "Flight, Six Salvadorans who took leave of the war," *The Progressive*, March 1983.

Harper's — "Can the U.S. Live with Latin Revolution?" Interviews with Central American experts, June 1984.

Christopher Hitches — "The Selling of Military Intervention," *The Nation*, August 20/27, 1983.

Irving Louis Horowitz — "Cuba and the Caribbean," *Worldview*, December 1983.

Eldon Kenworthy — "Central America: Beyond the Credibility Trap," *World Policy*, Fall 1983.

Peter Kornbluh — "U.S. Involvement in Central America: A Historical Lesson," *USA Today*, September 1983.

Walter LaFeber — "How We Make Revolutions Inevitable," *The Nation*, January 1984.

Ronald Reagan — "Central America: Defending Our Vital Interests," *Department of State Bulletin*, June 1983.

Ernesto Rivas-Gallont — "El Salvador: The Principle of Non-Intervention," *Vital Speeches of the Day*, October 15, 1981.

Kenneth E. Sharpe — "Facing Facts in El Salvador: Reconciliation or War," *World Policy Journal*, Spring 1984.

Is Communism a Threat in Central America?

"The communist program to conquer Central America must be defeated."

Communism Is a Threat in Central America

Fred Schwarz

Fred Schwarz is the president of the Christian Anti-Communism Crusade. The crusade operates in various cities and attempts to inform Americans of the philosophy, techniques, and strategy of Communism and associated forces. In the following viewpoint, Mr. Schwarz examines the situation in Central America and declares that the threat to Central America is Communism, not poverty or oppression.

As you read, consider the following questions:

1. How does Mr. Schwarz use the Pilgrims and Plymouth Rock as an example of incomplete statements?
2. What "consequences" are predictable if Marxist-Leninists conquer Central America, according to the author?
3. What in the author's opinion are the options for the US in Central America?

Fred Schwarz, "Who Is Creating Communists in Central America?" *Christian Anti-Communism Crusade*, July 15, 1983. Reprinted with permission.

Mark Dowie, editor of *Mother Jones* magazine, and I were guests on the Michael Dixon show on KCBS Radio Station of San Francisco. The program presented a true interchange of ideas. The host was impartial, perceptive and meticulously fair, while Mark Dowie was courteous, intelligent, and articulate. The absence of personal attacks enabled us to present and discuss our conflicting convictions.

Mark claimed that U.S. policies towards Fidel Castro, after the success of his Cuban Revolution, had forced him to turn to the Soviet Union and that this had been the cause of his embrace of communism. He contended that similar U.S. policies were forcing the Sandinistas of Nicaragua and other revolutionary groups in Central America to become communists. Thus, U.S. policies, while subjectively anti-communist, were objectively pro-communist. U.S. attitudes and programs were generating communists in ever-increasing numbers in the countries south of the border.

Mark argued that U.S. policies should be reversed. The U.S. should repudiate the anti-communist regimes which were dictatorial and oppressive and support the revolutionary forces which were seeking to overthrow tyrannical governments and improve the well-being of the common man. Such support would prevent these regimes from turning to the Soviet Union and embracing communism.

His point of view seemed to have much to commend it, and it is shared by a substantial number of the educated elite in this country. The important questions are: "Does he have a true interpretation of the existing situation? Would his advocated policies produce the results he promises?"

I pointed out that Fidel Castro had said: "I am a Marxist-Leninist, and have been one since my student days; but I hid it so that I could bring the revolution to a successful conclusion." Castro's confession that he had been a communist before the success of the revolution destroyed the validity of the argument that the treatment he had received from the U.S.A., following the success of the revolution, had driven him to communism.

Mark was unimpressed. He said that Castro and other people make all sorts of statements depending upon the occasion and circumstances. These statements often conflict and should be treated with appropriate reservations. He insisted that the observed facts confirmed that U.S. conduct had driven the Cuban revolution on to the communist pathway.

Mark claimed that the revolutions of Central and South America are caused by the intolerable conditions of poverty and oppression that prevail in those areas.

The premises which lead to these conclusions are not simply false. They are much more dangerous than that. They are incomplete and lead logically to conclusions which are false, but convincing, and which are believed with great sincerity.

Partial truth is often more dangerous than outright falsehood because it is more deceptive. The poet Tennyson said:

> A lie which is half a truth is the wickedest lie of all;
> For a lie which is all a lie can be met with and fought outright,
> But a lie which is half a truth is a harder matter to fight.

Which of the following statements, concerning the journey of the Pilgrims on the Mayflower to the shores of the new world at Plymouth Rock, are true?

1. They were driven to the new world by the winds and tides of the Atlantic.
2. They were driven to the new world by the cruelty and oppression of the authorities in England.
3. They were brought to the new world by their passionate desire to worship God according to the dictates of their own consciences.
4. Their journey was made possible by the construction and availability of the ship, the Mayflower.
5. Their arrival was due to the skill of the captain and the crew who navigated, steered and controlled the sails so that they brought the ship and its cargo to the chosen destination.

Each statement is true, but standing alone it is incomplete. Policies which are based on the assumption that one statement is the whole truth, and which ignore or deny the others, are likely

cc The Washington Times 1983, reprinted with permission.

to be erroneous and lead to catastrophe.

There is widespread resentment of the poverty and injustice that prevails throughout Central America. This resentment has existed as long as organized society has existed. It is comparable to the winds and the tides that sweep the Atlantic and which have existed from time immemorial. The winds and the tides did not bring settlers to the new world until there existed a Mayflower to transport them and skilled navigators and sailors to harness the winds and tides, as well as people willing and eager to risk the dangers of the journey. The destination was chosen by the Pilgrims and reached due to the knowledge and skill of the navigators and helmsmen, not by the undirected strength of the winds and tides alone.

The revolutions of Central America are not spontaneous uprisings of the masses against their oppression. They are the result of the existence of revolutionary organizations which skillfully harness the resentment and suffering of the people and use their strength and resources for guerrilla war.

Revolutionary Organizations

Consider the revolution in El Salvador. It is conducted by a political-military organization known as the Farabundo Marti National Liberation Front, the FMLN. The military operations are conducted by the Unified Revolutionary Directorate (DRU). If the revolution is successful, this organization will have the real power.

The political arm, the Democratic Revolutionary Front, the FDR, is based outside the country and is useful for propaganda purposes but has little real power.

The DRU is composed of five independent revolutionary organizations. These are:

1. The Popular Liberation Forces (FPL)
2. The People's Revolutionary Army (ERP)
3. The Armed Forces of National Resistance (FARN)
4. The Armed Forces of Liberation (FAL)
5. The Central American Workers Revolutionary Party (PRTC)

Each of these organizations was formed by an individual or a small group of individuals with passionate convictions. These convictions are held so strongly that disagreement often leads to the physical destruction of one of the contending parties. For example, the leaders of the FPL have just been engaged in policy conflicts which led to the murder and suicide of the top commanders.

The ERP is led by Joaquín Villalobos. In 1975, Villalobos personally executed his principal rival, a pro-Cuban poet named Roque Dalton, after accusing him of being a spy for both the Cubans and the CIA.

Each organization was created by a leader with Marxist-Leninist convictions. Most of these leaders were converted to communism while they were students. Literature, which was produced by the communists and distributed by teachers, played an important role in their conversion.

Consequently all the organizations follow the philosophy and doctrines of Marxism-Leninism. These guide the leaders as they decide on policies to follow during the revolutionary phase and will guide them in the formulation of policies and programs if the revolution is successful. Marxism-Leninism has preordained that the regimes established by successful revolutionary forces will be dedicated to the overthrow of the United States and to the triumph of communism throughout the world. Intelligent U.S. policies must take this into account.

Let's Thwart Communist Revolution

Central America. . . .is a region on the doorstep of the United States, and therefore demands a United States policy that above all promotes the democratic forces and practices there which alone can thwart communist revolution. The fact that US policies in the past helped create the very conditions which have spawned leftist revolutions does not mean that the US should not try by all reasonable means to stem a potential tide of Marxism in the region. What happens in Central America *is* strategically important, and, as long as there are democrats and moderates prepared to fight for economic reform and social justice, they deserve Washington's sustained help.

The Christian Science Monitor, August 29, 1983.

It is true that the conduct of individuals is influenced by the external conditions these individuals and organizations face. It is also true that their conduct is influenced by the beliefs which guide the individuals and organizations as they interpret the external conditions and devise policies in relation to them.

Any attempt to understand conduct without considering the beliefs which motivate that conduct is stupid. It will lead to a false interpretation of the present and an inaccurate prediction of the future. It is only possible to understand present actions and to predict future ones when we know the prevailing ideology which motivates present and future conduct. Policies based on assumptions which ignore the role of ideology are foredoomed to failure.

Can we affirm that Hitler's "final solution" was the result of

143

Jewish conduct and was not the result of the insane, but sincerely believed, convictions of Adolph Hitler concerning the evil nature of the Jews? The horrors of the gas chambers and incinerators of the holocaust were the product of the deadly ideas which were taught to Hitler and accepted by him.

Was the murder-suicide of over 900 people in the jungles of Guyana, when Jim Jones and his followers in the People's Church engaged in the orgy of self-destruction and murder, caused by the visit of Congressman Ryan and his party and not by the ideas in the disordered mind of Jim Jones? The coming of Congressman Ryan may have triggered the destruction, but the potentials for it already existed. The instruments of mass suicide had been prepared. The cyanide was ready. Rehearsals for mass suicide had been held. The beliefs in the mind of Jim Jones produced their harvest of destruction.

The doctrines of Marxism-Leninism are an important element in the revolutions in Central America. They must be given adequate attention when formulating policies.

Those who believe the doctrines of Marxism-Leninism—and this includes those who direct the guerrilla fighters—are convinced that the U.S.A. is "imperialistic". This leads inescapably to the conclusion that the U.S.A. is the enemy of their revolution and will seek to destroy it. Any friendliness and support given by the U.S.A. must, therefore, be designed to deceive the revolution. Only when the U.S.A. is destroyed will true peace be possible. Thus, hostility to the U.S.A. is foreordained by belief in the doctrine.

If the Marxist-Leninists conquer any country in Central America, certain consequences are predictable:

1. The hopes of the people in the area for democratic freedoms will vanish. A totalitarian dictatorship will be established.
2. The people of the conquered country will be militarized.
3. A system of universal espionage will be created.
4. Food production will decrease.
5. A host of refugees will try to flee the country.
6. A new base for the distribution of communist propaganda will be created.
7. The non-communist neighbors of that country will be endangered.
8. Another step in the encirclement of the U.S.A. will have been taken.

US Options in Central America

The U.S.A. is not confronted with the choice between giving unconditional support to an existing regime with a history of corruption and contempt for human rights and giving support to Marxist-Leninist revolutionaries. It can use its influence to persuade the existing authorities to institute genuine democratic and humane reforms. These include:

1. Holding elections in which the people can choose the individuals who they wish to govern them. For such elections to be genuinely democratic, the electors must be free to choose between a number of contending individuals and parties; and candidates must be able to campaign in security.
2. The establishment of a system of impartial justice so that crimes and corruption are punished even if the guilty hold high positions.
3. Support for programs to alleviate poverty, ignorance, illiteracy, and disease.

These reforms are made difficult by the depredations of the guerrillas and are impossible if the guerrillas win. Therefore, the guerrillas must be denied victory. Military assistance must be provided where this is necessary.

National Security Threat Real

There are no easy choices in Central America. Our decisions would be simpler if our friends there had perfect governments or if the rebellions were not supported by our adversaries. We could more easily afford to be morally fastidious if our security were not threatened by events in Central America. Alas, none of this is true—and our security is very much threatened.

Jack Kemp, *The New York Times*, July 29, 1983.

Programs to improve economic well-being are long-range. They must be accompanied by an aggressive truth campaign which distributes truthful information about:

1. The errors and fallacies of Marxist-Leninist doctrine.
2. The monopoly, dictatorship, brutality, and mass murder that has occurred in every country which the communists have conquered.
3. The true and undesirable objectives of the communists.

Such a campaign will:

1. Diminish the success of the communist campaign to recruit idealistic students.
2. Persuade some of the communists to discard their dangerous delusions.
3. Weaken the morale of the communist forces.

4. Preserve the opportunity to enlarge the domain of personal and national freedom.
5. Restore the reputation of the U.S.A. and thereby contribute to the security of this country.

The communist program to conquer Central America must be defeated.

"An obsessive, undifferentiated fear of communism governs present U.S. policy in Central and Latin America."

The Communist Threat in Central America Is Exaggerated

Robert Gomer

Robert Gomer is a professor of chemistry and director of the James Franck Institute at the University of Chicago. He earned a Ph.D. in chemistry from the University of Rochester and was AEC fellow in chemistry at Harvard. He is a member of the *Bulletin of Atomic Scientists* board of directors. In the following viewpoint, Mr. Gomer contends that the US should stop "opposing all revolutions automatically" because of its fear of communism.

As you read, consider the following questions:

1. How, according to Mr. Gomer does the US find itself "in the trap of supporting. . .the worst, most repressive and least viable regimes in the world"?
2. Why is attempting to establish democracies unrealistic, according to Mr. Gomer?
3. Does Mr. Gomer believe Central American revolutions will end up Communist? Why or why not?

Robert Gomer, "The United States and Central America," *Bulletin of the Atomic Scientists*, August/September 1983. Reprinted by permission of THE BULLETIN OF THE ATOMIC SCIENTISTS, a magazine of science and public affairs. Copyright © by the Educational Foundation for Nuclear Science, Chicago, IL 60637.

The United States has traditionally regarded Central and indeed much of Latin America as something of a fiefdom, a region where U.S. wishes and political and business interests could be flouted only at grave peril. Since the end of World War II the countries of Central America have been in the throes of social and political upheaval, affecting not only their internal affairs but also their relations with the United States.

Profound changes are inevitable and will occur whether we like it or not. Unfortunately, at a time when the pace of change is accelerating, and great wisdom on the part of the United States would be needed to influence Central America constructively, an Administration is in power in Washington determined not only to prevent all change but to turn back the clock wherever possible.

As in all foreign affairs, an obsessive, undifferentiated fear of communism governs present U.S. policy in Central and Latin America and leads the Administration to view any and all attempts to change the status quo as Moscow-inspired, Moscow-controlled, and therefore to be opposed at any price. It shuts its eyes resolutely to injustices and barbarities of enormous scale when they are committed by the regimes it succors and makes the only requirement for U.S. support a sufficiently rabid degree of anti-communism. To regimes like those in El Salvador or Guatemala any call for more social and economic justice is by definition communism, and this definition is not questioned by Washington. Thus we find ourselves in the trap of supporting in Central and Latin America some of the worst, most repressive and least viable regimes in the world.

Revulsion at US Support

In reaction to this policy there has been mounting revulsion by the public at our continued support of such brutal, corrupt and murderous regimes as those in El Salvador, Guatemala and Chile, and people are questioning whether we can maintain these in power for very long by any means. Despite growing dissatisfaction with current U.S. policy very little seems to have been said or written about the direction it should take.

Perhaps it is time to face this question with some honesty. Before addressing it let me try to answer a much easier one: What are the likely consequences of present U.S. policy? First, and perhaps most important, will be the loss of self-respect ensuing from the brutal and bloody pursuit of present aims, and demoralization when these aims turn out to be unachieveable. Our much-touted national will needs moral and rational underpinning, not the corpses of women and children.

A more immediate result of current U.S. policy is that it necessarily polarizes all attempts to overthrow regimes like that in El Salvador and practically forces revolutions into the arms of Moscow. Where else can revolutionaries look for support if the United States condemns them *a priori*? Once hardline Marxists have taken over a revolution, often thanks to U.S. policy, centrist factions are usually ground up, absorbed either into the far right or the far left, or simply exterminated by both sides.

Anti-Communism and Vietnam

It seems impossible that we can prop up for very long by force regimes that would crumble under their own weight of incompetence and corruption if we withdrew our support. At the very least we would have to keep a large U.S. military force permanently engaged in Central America, and probably would have to wage Vietnam-style scorched-earth campaigns, carpet bombings, defoliations of the jungle, burning of crops, herding of

Clay Bennet, *St. Petersburg Times*, reprinted with permission.

peasants into concentration camps and all the rest. Quite apart from the political impossibility (I hope) of such a course, there is no guarantee that it would work, or that it would not lead to really massive Soviet intervention and a general conflagration. It is hard to imagine even this Administration seriously considering such a course, although the logic of its actions to date certainly

149

points in that direction.

Short of all-out destruction of countries like El Salvador the most likely outcome of current U.S. policy is therefore to fulfill its own prophecies; that is, to ensure that the regimes which will come to power sooner or later will be totally hostile to the United States, totally dependent on Moscow, with no chance of breaking that dependence even if they wished to do so. One of the most serious consequences of this will be the resultant exacerbation of the conflict with the Soviet Union and the increased danger of nuclear war resulting from that.

What then should U.S. policy be in Central America? In my opinion the aim of establishing democratic governments, in our sense of the word, is no more realistic in the short term than trying to prop up fascist dictatorships and military juntas, which is what we are doing now. The social inequities, the enormous injustices of the past and present, a largely illiterate peasantry and, above all, the unwillingness of the ruling juntas of generals and land-owners to share their wealth and power make it very doubtful that democracy can be achieved soon, no matter who wins.

What can U.S. policy hope to accomplish? Should it push, in El Salvador for instance, for a dialogue between the incumbent regime and the rebels? Reagan's special envoy, former Senator Richard Stone, has recently voiced the belief that elections rather than dialogue are the answer, a view also offered by U.N. Ambassador Jeane Kirkpatrick. The kindest, if hardly the most accurate, interpretation of these statements is that they recognize the impossibility of dialogue; however, the same factors that make dialogue impossible also make meaningful elections unrealistic. Even if honest and free elections could be held, which is unlikely in the first place, would the military really abide by an outcome which favored even a moderate right-of-center government?

Economic Aid Wasteful

It has recently been suggested by Speaker of the House Thomas O'Neill that economic rather than military aid is the answer. If such aid is given to the incumbent regimes it will be a waste of money; almost nothing will trickle down to those who need help, and it would be more efficient to transfer the moneys directly to the relevant unmarked Swiss bank accounts of those in power now. Economic aid to Central America is certainly important and necessary but it cannot serve a useful function until less corrupt regimes have replaced present ones.

In my opinion current U.S. policy is launched fundamentally on the wrong tack and attempts at minor alterations of course, although an improvement on attempts to prop up the unproppable by naked force, are not going to work either. A sane U.S. policy must be based on the recognition that revolutions in Latin America come about because there is something to revolt about, not because Moscow and Havana have somehow convinced otherwise happy people to take the risk of getting killed and tortured for the sake of being a mite in Uncle Sam's eye.

We must further recognize that revolutions are usually led by revolutionaries and that these would probably be quite out of place at a Republican fund raiser. If only for want of a better label revolutionaries will frequently be called Marxists and think of themselves as Marxists although they are also nationalists. Our fatal mistake is to equate that with automatic subservience to the Soviet Union. It is not clear if a less rigid rejection of revolutions by the United States would or could keep them from being dominated by Marxists but, paradoxically, our only chance of preventing that is to shed our irrational fear of communism and stop opposing all revolutions automatically.

Communist Infiltration Is a Myth

The State Department has actively promoted as fact the myth that the Salvadoran guerrillas receive most of their weapons from Cuba and other communist countries. Although the tons of outside arms alleged in the administration's white paper on El Salvador sound massive, they actually constitute only a few days supplies. The guerrillas purchase most of their weapons on the black market with millions of dollars obtained in ransom.

Leonel Gomez and Bruce Cameron, *Foreign Policy*, Summer 1981.

Do we really know the course that Central American revolutions would eventually take if we left them alone or even helped them? All we can know for certain is that our present attitude forces them to depend on Moscow, radicalizes them, and must lead to ever more bloodshed and agony. If the victors turn out to be Marxists we should recognize that we can not only live with them, but can, by virtue of our geographic and economic position, exert considerable influence and serve as a very effective counterweight to Soviet influence. One need only look at Southeast Asia, or Eastern Europe for that matter, to realize that communist countries are not totally happy to be dominated by Moscow or Peking and, geography permitting, would prefer to steer their own courses.

Perhaps it is too much to ask for this country to remember its own revolutionary past and actively aid some of the revolutions now in progress or soon to occur in Latin America; but it should not be too much to ask for the United States to be at least neutral, and not to come down automatically on the wrong side. In the long run that is the only policy which can ensure us a reasonable role in the region and can produce stability rather than continued turmoil. In our relations with Latin America less would be much more.

How likely is such a change in U.S. policy? There are mounting signs of dissatisfaction with the Administration's policy but no signs that moderates in Congress are ready to formulate anything even vaguely along the lines suggested here. Moderates in Congress feel impaled on the horns of a dilemma. They cannot in good conscience support the Administration's present policy but dare not come out strongly for non-interference, for fear of later being blamed for "losing" Central America, as a previous generation was blamed for "losing" China. However, not to speak out firmly and openly against a policy that makes no sense is precisely the form of political cowardice most likely to reap its just rewards. If Congress does not come out strongly and convincingly against the present policy and continues to hedge its bets by giving it lukewarm, strings-attached support, it will most surely be blamed for the eventual failure of that policy anyway. Affixing blame to others for such failures is what Mr. Reagan excels at. If it were not for the thousands of lives unnecessarily lost and the serious long term consequences for all of us this would serve the trimmers right. As it is, we can only hope that a greater measure of wisdom and courage than we are accustomed to seeing in Congress will somehow emerge before it is too late.

"The militarily powerful Sandinista party has imposed on Nicaraguans a. . .tyranny of violence and oppression."

The Sandinistas Are a Totalitarian Threat

Esther Wilson

Esther Wilson is a policy analyst for the Heritage Foundation. She has a B.A. from Mary Washington College and an M.A. in foreign affairs from the University of Virginia. Having lived in Argentina and El Salvador, she is a specialist in Argentine politics. In the following viewpoint, Ms. Wilson explains how she believes the Sandinista government in Nicaragua has not fulfilled its promises to improve the lives of the Nicaraguan people.

As you read, consider the following questions:

1. Does the author believe freedom of speech, assembly and private property exist in Nicaragua?
2. Is the Catholic Church being undermined, according to Ms. Wilson?
3. Does the author believe that the US should support the contra opposition to the Nicaraguan government?

Esther Wilson, "The Battle for Democracy in Central America," *The Backgrounder*, March 14, 1984. Reprinted with permission of The Heritage Foundation, 214 Massachusetts Ave. NE, Washington, DC 20002.

Much has been said and written about the Sandinista government and its efforts to change the economic and political system of Nicaragua. Little has been noted of the many disillusioned men and women who fought alongside the Sandinistas to overthrow Anastasio Somoza, because they believed that they were building a new democratic order. Using methods all too familiar, the militarily powerful Sandinista party has imposed on Nicaraguans a worse tyranny of violence and repression. This has driven many one-time allies of the Sandinistas into opposition once again—this time against the government run by the Marxist-Leninist FSLN (Sandinista National Liberation Front). This opposition includes the freedom fighters or the "Contras," the Catholic Church, the one nongovernment newspaper, *La Prensa*, the private sector, and the Indians, who are calling for a democratic system and freedom from oppression.

Nicaraguans' freedom of speech, assembly, and private property have almost ceased to exist. Yet some nonsupporters of the Sandinistas, who have not overlooked or rationalized Sandinista repression, portray the democratic opposition in Sandinista terms as "Somocistas" or "the right-wing opposition," when in fact the representatives of this opposition are primarily liberal democrats who for years opposed the Somoza regime. . . .

Internal Political Opposition

An important political organization inside Nicaragua is the Democratic Coordinating Board. Under the leadership of Eduardo Rivas Gasteozoro, internationally recognized for his human rights campaign against Somoza, the Coordinating Board is composed of several political parties, businessmen, and union representatives. Its function is to negotiate on behalf of its members for the right to continue their work and to participate in the elections.

Like many other groups and individuals in Nicaragua, the Democratic Coordinating Board hopes that, by staying and fighting within the system created by the Sandinistas, they will make democratic gains. . . .

The Private Sector

Important as a political opposition group is COSEP, the Nicaraguan Higher Council of the Private Sector. COSEP represents those Nicaraguan businesses that have not been fully nationalized. Like other opposition groups and organizations, COSEP is allowed to exist, but is denied access to the media, and attacked in the government newspapers, television and radio stations. Many of its members have been physically assaulted by mobs, and in numerous cases, imprisoned without being charged. Although the government recently invited the representatives to participate in a dialogue, COSEP's demands and criticisms were barred from distribution, and the efforts of the one independent newspaper, *La Prensa*, to print the demands were stopped by the government. . . .

COSEP's newly elected president, Enrique Bolaños, has requested permission from the Sandinistas to sponsor programs daily on the radio and weekly on television to discuss political and economic topics. Skeptical that his request will be granted, Bolanos observes: "There was a time when we thought we could make the Sandinistas come fairly close to their original programs. But now they have made very clear that they are Marxist-Leninists who are moving towards creating a totalitarian state.". . .

The Catholic Church

Just as the Catholic Church in Nicaragua under the leadership of Archbishop Obando y Bravo opposed the repression of the Somoza dictatorship, it now opposes the repression under the Sandinistas. As a result, it has become a major target of Sandinista propaganda and government sponsored mob attacks. In the last three months, 22 churches have been attacked by gangs, who set tires afire outside the churches and threatened those trying to enter to pray. The Bishop himself has been harassed and attacked on his way to services.

Steve Kelley, *San Diego Union*, reprinted with permission.

The new Archbishop Pablo Antonio Vega Mantilla was expected to be less political. Yet he has stated that the Catholic Church "...[is] not a political opposition, we are believers in any regime based on Christian values. In Nicaragua today people feel an excessive control and are unable to realize their full potential." He added, "much of the creative dynamism of the revolution has been lost, it has been replaced by scheme imposed from the outside."

The Sandinistas appreciate the church's powerful influence. They have tried to undermine this power by creating a "People's Church." But this "is more fiction than reality," Arturo Cruz, an ex-member of the junta, writes in *Foreign Affairs*.

The Catholic Church is prohibited from receiving funds or contributions from abroad. The Archbishop's Sunday Mass no longer is televised. The People's Church, on the other hand, is heavily funded from abroad, particularly by Protestant and Catholic churches in the United States, and has its own television and radio stations.

Most recently, the Catholic Church has protested the Sandinista's efforts to take over the nongovernment Catholic schools. The Episcopal Conference of Bishops, which governs the Catholic Church in Nicaragua, is backing fully the La Salle Order of Teachers' refusal to replace the traditional curriculum with Marxist-Leninist teachings. *La Prensa*, which tried to report the story on January 27, was closed down by the government. Archbishop Pablo Antonio Vega, President of the Nicaraguan Episcopal Conference, has stated that "at this time in Nicaragua there is not a state of law, or basis for liberty and democracy." Like the other groups in the opposition, the Episcopal Conference has demanded of the government fulfillment of its original promise of nonalignment, popular sovereignty, suggesting that "the people be the subject not the object of the revolution."

The Press

La Prensa, the only remaining nongovernment newspaper, is censored daily. In fact, the Sandinistas have set up a special office exclusively to censor *La Prensa*, according to editor Violeta Chamorro, who was a member of the Junta until 1981. The Sandinistas cannot shut the paper down completely. It would cost too much politically not only because *La Prensa* still symbolizes, after many years of struggle against Somoza, the fight against tyranny to Nicaraguans and much of the world, but also because the Sandinistas would no longer be able to credibly assert that freedom of the press exists in Nicaragua. *La Prensa* is internationally known for its opposition to Somoza, and the assassination of its editor Edgar Chamorro, Violeta's husband, was the turning point of world opinion against Somoza.

The Sandinistas do not limit their press control to censorship. Most of the attacks, according to the editors, occur outside the editorial offices. Distributors are often attacked by government mobs, some have been jailed by the government, their families threatened, and their houses painted with derogatory slogans. *La Prensa*'s editorial council has taken an active political stand before the Sandinista Government. It recently demanded fulfillment of points 4 and 5 of the Contadora Group's proposals, which call for the establishment of pluralistic democratic regimes in Central America.

America's Objective in Nicaragua

In Nicaragua, we are not giving sufficient support to the guerrilla forces that are opposing a rigid Marxist leadership that is destroying democracy in that nation. The support we are giving the rebels, despite doubts expressed by leftist elements, seems designed more to discourage Nicaragua's support for guerrilla forces in El Salvador than to open up Nicaragua to national reconciliation, pluralistic government and free elections. Surely the latter should be the American objective.

If we want to win, we must have the courage to do what is needed rather than merely to attempt to paper over an untenable situation.

Morton Kaplan, *The Washington Times*, November 17, 1983.

In recent weeks, the Sandinistas claim to have eased the censorship of *La Prensa*. Yet the paper has been closed down twice more since it attempted to print the statements of the Episcopal Conference of Bishops.

Labor Unions

Nearly extinct, the remaining nongovernment labor unions are struggling to stay alive with the help of the Nicaraguan Higher Council of Private Enterprise and the Democratic Coordinating Board. These free unions, the Workers Central (CTN) and the Confederation for Labor Unification (CUS), both of which opposed the Somoza government, have suffered from an unrelenting government campaign of repression. Their members have been assaulted by mobs, arrested and beaten, and their families are threatened. The leaders have been forbidden to hold meetings, collect dues, bargain without government intervention, hold seminars, organize, or leave the country without explicit permission from the Council of Ministers.

Although the members of the various opposition groups inside Nicaragua have not publicly endorsed the armed opposition of the FDN and the ARDE, they have not condemned it. Many of their spokesmen concede that, with the focus of the Sandinistas constantly diverted to the external opposition, the internal opposition has more room for maneuvering. Many feel that, without external pressure, the Sandinista government never would have been compelled to issue its peace proposals last December, which promised more freedom and political and economic opportunities to the opposition groups and other members of Nicaraguan society as well as announced elections. In addition, the various opposition groups have unanimously asserted the right of the leaders or representatives of FDN and ARDE to participate in the upcoming elections.

Implications for US Policy

The ruling Sandinista directorate was never elected. It came to power only by its alliance with the truly democratic and popular opposition to Somoza. It has maintained its power only through force. By aligning itself with the Soviet bloc, where free elections never are held and power is maintained through terror, the Sandinista regime has made clear the undemocratic path it has chosen. And were it not for the large and growing presence of Soviet and Cuban personnel and armaments in Nicaragua, the armed opposition of the Contras would not need U.S. assistance.

The U.S. government should continue supporting the armed opposition. Through this pressure and through diplomatic channels, the U.S. can support the democratic demands of the internal opposition as well. The U.S. government can aid in the democratic opening of Nicaragua by publishing opposition demands at the United Nations and the Organization of American States as a counterpoint to Nicaraguan demands on the U.S.

Costa Rica, which has no army, is especially vulnerable to Sandinista and Mexican pressure to cease supporting the Contras who receive supplies and find refuge inside Costa Rican borders. Costa Rica's insecurity should not be exacerbated by a wavering U.S. policy. U.S. support for the democratic Contra forces should be continued as part of a firm U.S. stance. So should financial aid, and military aid when requested, to Nicaragua's increasingly apprehensive neighbors. Without U.S. strength behind them, the choice will be narrowed to those forces inside their respective governments that offer "peace" only through accommodation.

Finally, the OAS and the world should be reminded of the Sandinistas' promises to the OAS in July of 1979 that have never been fulfilled and as a result are now the basis of the opposition's demands. As the Sandinistas were able through those democratic commitments to receive the recognition of their legitimacy as a government, then this legitimacy, at the very least, should be called into question by the representatives at the OAS and other international organizations.

Conclusion

Although politically diverse, the several elements of the Nicaraguan democratic opposition share the principal objective of achieving the democratic goals of the revolution of 1979 that overthrew Anastasio Somoza.

The Sandinista government's charge that the opposition represents the old Somoza regime is unfounded. The small minority of ex-National Guardsmen active within the FDN are not politically important and are not part of the leadership. There are, in fact, former members of the Somoza government now in the Sandinista regime and many former National Guardsmen in the Sandinista security forces. Most important, substantial progress has been made toward an alliance between the Nicaraguan Democratic Forces and the Democratic Revolutionary Alliance.

In 1979, international support of the anti-Somoza revolution was made possible through the presence of the democratic opposition within the Sandinista movement. The Sandinistas rode to power on their backs. Now this same opposition, divided into political and military camps, is fighting the takeover of their country by totalitarian forces. The struggle is not between Somocistas and the people; it is between democracy and communist totalitarianism. By supporting the opposition forces, the United States is squarely on the side of democracy.

"The changes in the internal life of Nicaragua have served to make the nation a sign and transmitter of hope to many Latin American countries where the poor are exploited."

The Sandinistas Are Not a Totalitarian Threat

World Council of Churches

The World Council of Churches is an ecumenical fellowship of various religious denominations in over 100 countries. Headquartered in Geneva, Switzerland, it focuses on Christian unity, inter-church aid, mission and evangelism, laity work, and assistance to developing countries. It also conducts extensive refugee and resettlement programs around the world. In the following viewpoint, the Delegation to Nicaragua expresses its support for the advances the Sandinistas have made in the lives of the Nicaraguan people and finds US criticism of the Sandinistas unfounded.

As you read, consider the following questions:

1. According to the authors, is Nicaragua "engaged in acts of military aggression against its neighbors"?
2. Do the authors believe the Catholic Church is being undermined in Nicaragua?
3. In the author's opinion, should the US aid the Sandinista government?

"Report to the World Council of Churches of its Delegation Sent to Nicaragua," *Catholicism in Crisis*, January 1984. Reprinted with permission of the World Council of Churches, 150, Route de Ferney, Geneva, Switzerland.

It is not necessary here to rehearse the historical antecedents of Nicaragua's recent history—the forty years of Somoza domination and exploitation, and the immense efforts since then to rebuild the nation as a new society. Rather we share some reflections on what we saw and heard in Nicaragua during our brief visit.

A. Nicaragua is a nation under severe military attack, suffering frequent aggressions on both its northern and southern borders. Military incursions are made into Nicaragua to sow terror, to kill civilians, to disrupt normal life and sometimes to capture the population of whole villages taken back beyond the borders of the country. Our delegation talked with persons whose family members had been killed or injured, with persons displaced by the attacks, and we saw ample evidence on the Honduras border of the damage resulting from such attacks. Most dramatically, as our delegation was proceeding to the Managua airport on the morning of September 8, to fly to Puerto Cabezas on the Atlantic Coast, the airport was bombed and a strafing attack was directed at the home of the Minister of Foreign Affairs, Father Miguel D'Escoto and which seriously endangered a large church school. This state of virtual war against Nicaragua is the major reality the nation contends with today. It influences the entire life of the nation, it creates and prolongs unnecessary human suffering, it disrupts economic planning and development, and has rendered normal life impossible. One result has been the proposed institution of compulsory military service (Servício Militar Patriótico). As Christians we decry the human tragedy being visited upon Nicaragua.

Military Aggression Supported by US

It is well known that the widespread military aggression against Nicaragua, in which members of Somoza's infamous National Guard as well as others participate, is amply supported by the Government of the United States, as the United States ambassador confirmed for us. The United States has also introduced at least four thousand combat troops into Honduras, menacing Nicaragua's northern border further. Beyond any internal conflict, Nicaragua is the object of a well-orchestrated and massively funded effort of an international character to bring down the present Nicaraguan revolutionary government and to institute in its stead a government more acceptable to the United States. As a delegation we repudiate this aggression in the strongest terms and call for the prompt cessation of United States intervention, whether direct or indirect, whether overt or covert.

B. One of the reasons often cited for the attacks on Nicaragua is that it receives much assistance from the U.S.S.R. and Cuba—cultural, economic, technical and military. In addition, it is charged that the Nicaraguan government has facilitated the shipment of arms to the El Salvador guerrilla forces. With reference to the support from the U.S.S.R. and Cuba there is no doubt that Nicaragua has received considerable assistance from those nations, as well as from many other countries of the world, socialist, western and non-aligned. This is readily acknowledged, indeed Nicaragua deliberately wishes to move away from its overwhelming erstwhile dependence on the United States alone in order to achieve a "diversity dependency" on many nations so that it will not be overly subject to any one nation. Nevertheless, we know of no evidence that would indicate that external assistance from any source has been used in any way for aggressive attacks across Nicaragua's border on neighboring nations. The current aggression is clearly a one-way aggression, against Nicaragua.

As for the presumed military support of opposition forces in El Salvador, there is no doubt that the Sandinista government supports the goals of those who struggle against the present El Salvador government, but we find it remarkable that very little, if any, hard evidence has been forthcoming about military

"Ain't nobody here but us Nicaraguans . . . !"

Marlette, *The Charlotte Observer*, reprinted with permission.

assistance from those who loudly denounce it, despite their access to sophisticated electronic monitoring devices. One would expect those who make such charges to provide clear and copious evidence of their existence, but apparently no such evidence exists.

The fact is that Nicaragua is not engaged in acts of military aggression against its neighbors, much as it might wish to see revolutionary governments such as its own in those countries.

C. There is also an important diplomatic context within which Nicaragua is attempting to solve present conflicts by negotiation, and not by military means. Most hopeful seem to be the efforts of the "Contadora" countries (Mexico, Panama, Venezuela, Colombia) to defuse the present military confrontation, and to secure the withdrawal of all foreign military assistance, from whatever source, to the area. The United States says it is supportive of the Contadora process, but even as it affirms this it is rapidly escalating military assistance to the "contras" (the term used by Nicaraguans to describe counter-revolutionary organizations in Honduras and Costa Rica currently attacking Nicaragua), and it is displaying large shows of military force in the oceans off both Nicaraguan coasts. We find such actions to be flat contradictions of the professed peaceful intentions of the United States and of the presumed support of the Contadora process. We urge that the United States immediately reverse these aggressive actions and give abundant signs, by concrete actions, of its support of Contadora. We believe that if the United States would begin withdrawal, the Contadora process would be greatly encouraged and peace could come at an early date to the region. All agree that the Contadora process is difficult and involved, but the United States holds the key to unlocking all major difficulties and to facilitate an early agreement. As Nicaraguan leaders said to us, what should evolve is a "peace created, not a peace imposed."

Nicaragua's Living Conditions Improved

D. Internally, Nicaragua is the scene of many encouraging developments, even in the midst of enormous difficulties. In the areas of literacy, education, health and housing, to name but a few, great strides have been taken to meet the vast needs of a population long subject during Somoza days to gross poverty, ignorance and exploitation. Many of Nicaragua's difficulties, though to be sure not all, are precipitated by the external aggression. The attempt of the Sandinista government, as we perceive it, is not, as it is often alleged to establish a Marxist state. Though there are undoubtably Marxists in governmental circles, what impresses us is the pluralism in the government, the service of Christians lay and clergy, at every level of government, and the sense we get that the kind of totalitarianism so rampant in many countries of Latin America (e.g. Chile, Uruguay, Guatemala, El Salvador) simply does not exist in Nicaragua.

What we see is a government faced with tremendous problems, some seemingly insuperable, bent on a great experiment which, though precarious and incomplete at many points, provides hope to the poor sectors of society, improves the conditions of education, literacy and health and for the first time offers the Nicaraguan people a modicum of justice for all rather than a society offering privilege exclusively to the wealthy, foreign and domestic large investors, and to the powerful in the state. The government has indeed exercised an option for the poor which has led to great improvements in the standard of life of the poor majority, even though the once-privileged elite minority now is not able to maintain the standards it once enjoyed at the expense of the majority. . . .

The changes in the internal life of Nicaragua have served to make the nation a sign and transmitter of hope to many Latin American countries where the poor and the exploited yearn for the kind of gains Nicaragua is achieving. In contrast to the charges that Nicaragua is trying to export its revolution elsewhere, what we see in Nicaragua is an internal reality that by its very existence and nature indicates that such improvements are possible and thereby provides great hope to nations where such gains yet remain unachieved.

We know that no state is perfect, as Nicaraguan leaders fully agree. We have explored some of the more frequent criticism of the Sandinista government. For example, charges are levelled that the Sandinista government hinders the free life of political parties. We believe there is some truth to this charge, though we also believe that steps being taken towards the scheduled 1985 elections (such as the law recently adopted on political parties) are highly encouraging. We were pleased to hear of some very recent public meetings of opposition parties without governmental interference. Another often repeated charge is that the press is censored. Since the declaration of a State of Emergency in March, 1982, this censorship has been in force. We were shown some of the censored material by *La Prensa*, a major opposition newspaper, and believe that some of the censorship has been excessive, even silly. We were glad to hear from a very high government official that he too considers the censorship excessive and that steps must be taken to reduce it. Though we are supporters of a free press, we can understand some of the particularities of Nicaragua that argue for the present censorship. At a period of intense external aggression which profoundly affects human lives, it is understandable that some control is deemed necessary in the face of all-too-often irresponsible press statements. We must add, however, that we are impressed by the internal press freedom that does exist (unlike the situation in many totalitarian countries) so that day in and day out a newspaper such as *La Prensa* can publish articles which explicitly and implicitly criticize the government. It is notable that *La*

Prensa apparently has nothing to say against the external aggression, thus raising questions about where its fundamental loyalties lie.

There have also been accusations that there is, or has been, religious persecution in Nicaragua. Some incidents of such "persecution" has been loudly touted in the foreign press. Our understandings, received from persons of various faiths, is that there is complete freedom of worship in Nicaragua. The few incidents that have been alleged as examples of persecution are isolated, some of them quite ambiguous in their meaning, and some patently false. What surprised us, as we brought up the matter of religious persecution in Nicaragua, was that highly respected observers spoke of a kind of "persecution" within the Roman Catholic Church itself, directed by the hierarchy against clergy who were not in accord with the hierarchy's opposition to the government, often resulting in forced removals of clergy from their parishes with no advance notice. A most recent example that refutes the charge of religious persecution by the government is the ample publication of, and comment on, the Statement of the Roman Catholic Episcopal Conference (dated August 29, 1983) strongly attacking the proposed law on compulsory military service, in effect urging Catholics to disobey the law.

Nicaraguans Trying to Survive

While the U.S. government now does everything it can to subvert revolutionary Nicaragua, Americans go down and give everything they've got to make it work properly. Nicaraguans don't fail to see the irony of this. They continually make a distinction between the American government and the American people—chastising the one and welcoming the other. . . .

From their point of view they had no choice but to go to the Soviet Union for aid, credit, machines, tractors, wheat, for things that they had previously gotten from the United States. And they sought Soviet arms to prepare for what they see as an imminent invasion by U.S. troops.

Peter Leyden, *St. Paul Dispatch,* August 10, 1983.

That such a statement can be widely published is hardly a sign of religious persecution of the church, though to be sure the Statement has been severely attacked by those supportive of the government. Nevertheless, unlike what might happen in some other societies, the authors of the Statement have not been jailed or otherwise molested.

E. Economically, Nicaragua has maintained a mixed economy, wherein private enterprise controls a larger share of the economy than does the public sector, though within the overall economic guidelines and policies set by the state. It is remarkable that, despite the immense economic problems Nicaragua inherited from Somoza and despite the external aggression, Nicaraguan economic life has shown many indications of improvement, as judged by statistics provided by the World Bank and other international financial institutions. . . . The prospects for 1983 look quite good, with an anticipated substantial gain in the Gross National Product, though the exact dimension of that gain remains to be seen. All of this has occurred as the international financial community has carried on a very systematic war against Nicaragua, closing down credits and markets, so it is not surprising that the economy faces difficulties. In many ways, as we were told, Nicaragua is forced into an economy of survival rather than an economy of development. What impresses us is that the economic policies of the nation are aimed at improvement of the conditions of the poorest sectors of society, even if the once privileged elites now must do with less, a fact about which they greatly complain. There are some food shortages in remote areas and economic dislocations but overall it seems to us that the ruinous economic picture presented abroad of Nicaragua is highly prejudicial and deceptive. It is of special interest that there has been a great increase in the demand for basic commodities in the nation because of the increase in the standard of living of the poor majority, a fact which indicates a major economic gain even as it explains some of the shortages. In any case, the most serious problem for the economy at present is external military aggression. If that were terminated there is every reason to believe that the Nicaraguan economy could recover fully and flourish.

Christians in Nicaragua

One of the most outstanding aspects of the Nicaraguan situation has been the intensive participation of Christians as individuals, as basic communities, and as churches in the revolution, before the overthrow of Somoza in July, 1979, and since. Historically this has been a unique thing. One of the popular slogans of the revolution, which we heard shouted repeatedly and saw painted on house walls, is that "Between Christianity and revolution there is no contradiction." As with any slogan, that is simplistic, but still indicative of a view of the relationship of faith and life one seldom witnesses nationally. Many Nicaraguans believe that their revolutionary process embodies basic Christian principles of love, concern for the poor, justice for all, and respect for human dignity. Christians in large numbers have seen a link between their faith, their Scriptures and their ethical behavior, and the struggle for a new and more just society.

166

In Latin America the Roman Catholic Church has proclaimed a "preferential option for the poor" which the new Nicaragua has truly attempted to embody. . . .

The Roman Catholic Church is increasingly divided between those who oppose the revolutionary process and those who still strongly support it. The former group includes Archbishop Miguel Obando y Bravo and some, though not all, of the nine Nicaraguan bishops, as well as lay persons principally coming from the more well-to-do families. The latter group is what has been called "the popular church" or "the church of the people," mostly poor and representative of workers and peasant groups.

Ideological Blinkers

It would be silly to assert that the government of Nicaragua is perfect. But if, as we and many others have concluded, it is a basically honest attempt to improve the life of the people, we should not let our ideological blinkers allow us to tolerate a dirty war against this independent country.

Nor can we remain silent while it happens. Yoachim Prinz, rabbi of Berlin under Hitler, once said, "The most important thing I learned in my life, under those tragic circumstances, is that bigotry and hatred are not the main problems. The most urgent and disgraceful, the most shameful, is silence."

Karen King and Chris Moss, *The Other Side*, May 1984.

The hierarchy, as well as the Pope during his recent visit to Nicaragua, have emphasized obedience to the bishops, apparently fearful that many Catholics do not respond sufficiently to the magisterial authority of the church. Behind this attitude there is an ecclesiology in Roman Catholicism with a concept of authority which the people's church seems to challenge. Those who represent the people's church do not want to engage in head-on confrontation with episcopal authority, but their reading of Scripture, as well as their revolutionary experience, leads them to see authority as emanating out of identification with the people's struggle. . . . We find it highly encouraging that in Nicaragua there are some excellent new expressions of ecumenical life, both among Protestant groups of quite varied theological backgrounds (CEPAD is the outstanding example) as well as between some Protestant and some Roman Catholic groups, often at the local level. . . .

There is at this time a sharp visible escalation of military aggression against Nicaragua which brings death, damage and great suffering to the people. In addition, economic, diplomatic and political moves are being taken to isolate, weaken and "destabilize" the country while false and distorted reports on the nature, intention and activities of the government, the churches, and people of Nicaragua are being circulated which serve these political efforts to discredit the leadership of the country and indeed in some cases to eliminate them. In the light of this dangerous situation which brings grave consequences for the hopes of justice and peace in the region, we urgently recommend that the WCC and the churches:

• Give immediate, tangible and visible support to the work of the churches in the United States, as they mobilize effective opposition to the present policies of their government toward Central America.

• Press governments for a negotiated political solution to the crisis in Nicaragua and Central America, while opposing United States military support to repressive and destabilizing governments and forces in the region, particularly through Honduras and Costa Rica.

• Encourage governments to increase state aid and credit to the Nicaraguan government for its social, economic and cultural programmes and projects, work for a resumption of significant international financial loans to Nicaragua and for an increase of private trade and activity, while urging the churches and their agencies to increase financial grants for ecumenically sponsored and supported projects benefiting the population.

• Throw every effort into the current peace initiatives being undertaken by Latin American states to reach agreement, through dialogue, on a stable and lasting peace based on legitimate national interests and justice concerns in the Central American region.

• Initiate and strengthen major efforts in the area of providing and disseminating information about Nicaragua, giving priority to the media and its potential ability to influence political and public opinion worldwide. . . .

• Seek and send material, human and financial resources for programmes of humanitarian assistance carried out among refugees and other sectors of the populations affected by repressive regimes of the Central American region. Particular attention should be given to the needs arising from the constant attacks on the lives and economic activities of the populations living in the border areas of Nicaragua.

"It is easier for a country with a predominant Latin Catholic ethic. . .to move from a right-wing government to a Marxist one rather than to a democratic one."

Marxism Is Natural to Central America

Yenny Nun

Yenny Nun is a lawyer and co-author of *Latin American Laws and Institutions.* A correspondent for the Chilean magazine *Cosas,* she divides her time between Santiago and Los Angeles. In the following viewpoint, Ms. Nun explains why Central American countries, with no history of democracy, more naturally lean toward Marxism.

As you read, consider the following questions:

1. What political principles have influenced Latin America, according to Ms. Nun?
2. Does Ms. Nun think democracy can take hold in Central America? Why or why not?

Yenny Nun, "Why Marxism Appeals to the Latin Nations," originally published in the October 11, 1983 issue of *The Los Angeles Times.* Reprinted with permission of the author.

Political structures in Latin America are in a state of profound change, and not since the Cuban Revolution has the United States been so worried about the spread of Marxism in the hemisphere. Before any strategy can be formulated to deal with that threat, the people and the policy-makers of the United States must understand this about Latin America: It is easier for a country with a predominant Latin Catholic ethic and no tradition of democracy to move from a right-wing government to a Marxist one rather than to a democratic one.

Latin America has for centuries been strongly influenced by feudal medieval Catholic values that are very similar to Marxist principles. The internalizing of these values—paternalism, authoritarianism, centralism and dogmatism among them—has resulted in a majority of authoritarian governments and varying degrees of anti-capitalistic economic behavior and social immobility in most of Spain's former colonies.

Every Latin American country on gaining independence promised to have "democratic institutions," yet few have managed to establish truly democratic governments. Each, for instance, has a constitution—but in most cases it's one of a succession of constitutions, some of which were superseded before ever taking effect.

US Constitution Original

Of course, one cannot compare the longevity and effectiveness of the U.S. Constitution to those of Latin America; still, one can wonder why the disparity is so remarkable. The people of the United States forget that their Constitution was an original creation by and for America's colonizers, ideally compatible with their needs and flexible enough to adapt to the needs of the future nation. The colonizers, while rejecting England's monarchy, retained much of its democratic political tradition, which had already been several centuries in evolving.

By contrast, Latin America's colonial period served to strengthen its dependence on Spain, where the tradition was a wedding of church and crown. As these colonies reached nationhood in the early 19th Century, they looked to foreign models—notably those of the United States and France—in constructing their constitutional charters. But the revolutionary American and French models' principles were incompatible with the deeply internalized ethic of Latin Catholicism.

In some cases (Chile, Uruguay, Colombia and Mexico) original constitutional ideals eventually were adapted to what could work in reality. But most of the new nations acceded to authoritarian government, whether military or civilian, and democratic tradition thus failed to develop.

The entrenchment of authoritarianism, paternalism and centrism has been strongest in Central America. There the new nations were governed by a handful of powerful families and dictators, a situation that the United States took advantage of to serve its own political and economic interests. The result was a region of nations without civic tradition. (The exceptions: Costa Rica, which managed to develop democratically by not having a standing army, and Mexico, which excluded the church from government affairs and sanctified the voters' role, albeit in a one-party system.)

Democracy a Foreign Entity

If there is to be any hope for U.S.-Central American relations, then certain realities must be considered. First, democracy as we know it is as foreign to Central Americans today as it was when Honduras's Francisco Morazan (the "George Washington of Central America") sought to unify the newly independent republics of the isthmus under a single constitutional confederation more than 150 years ago. We will never find the mirror image of American democracy in Central America because Latinos have always responded more readily to individuals than to ideologies. *Caudillismo*, strong oneman rule, was shaped by a history of Indian chieftains, flamboyant conquistadors, Spanish viceroys, inspired guerrilla fighters and dictators of every conceivable stripe. It is a tradition held together, ultimately, by the sheer force of personality. It links men of such ideological persuasions as Montezuma, Hernán Cortés, Morazan, Augusto César Sandino, Anastasio Somoza and Pope John Paul II.

William Lewis, *Newsweek*, December 19, 1983.

When popular discontent erupted in countries with no tradition of real popular participation in government, Marxism came to be seen by many as the "liberating" force. U.S.-style democracy was associated with support of the old authoritarian "oppressors." Even if U.S.-style democracy could be considered, it would be too revolutionary, requiring a complete change of centuries-old attitudes. Marxism, on the other hand, with its authoritarian, paternalistic and dogmatic style so similar to the characteristics of traditional Latin Catholicism, doesn't represent much of a change in people's prevalent ethic.

Where democratic traditions have been given some time to evolve, the key to their durability is their adherence to bans on military and church participation in government. Of all these nations, Chile has the longest tradition of continuous democratic government. This is why Chileans have been able to experiment with a Marxist leadership, survive the current authoritarian military regime and, now, exert strong pressure on the military to return to democracy.

But it must be remembered that "democrats" in Latin America are closer in style to those who have emerged in "Latin" Europe—in France, Italy, Spain and Portugal. Many of these leaders of Eurocommunism have rejected capitalist democracy because it is incompatible with their societies' internalized religious values. In attempting to solve this existential problem, some political minds have moved from Catholicism to Marxism, and some theologians have brought Marxism to Catholicism.

With patience the United States must accept the fact that its neighbors will have governments reflecting their ethics and national characteristics. And when the choice is democracy, it will not eliminate the deep undercurrents pushing these regimes to either the authoritarian right or the authoritarian left.

"The advance of Marxist states must be halted and reversed."

Marxism Must Be Stopped in Central America

Michael Novak

Michael Novak, theologian and philosopher, is a resident scholar in philosophy and public policy at the American Enterprise Institute. A prolific conservative writer, his articles appear in journals such as *Christianity & Crisis* and *National Review*. He is the author of several books including *Belief and Unbelief, The Rise of the Unmeltable Ethnics,* and *The Joy of Sports.* In the following viewpoint, Mr. Novak explains why Marxism is a negative, quasi-religious force and must be thwarted.

As you read, consider the following questions:

1. Does Mr. Novak support the idea that we should appease Marxist revolution in Central America? Why or why not?
2. What should US policy be in Central America, according to Mr. Novak?

Michael Novak, "Tomorrow and Tomorrow," *National Review,* July 22, 1983. © 1983 by National Review, Inc., 150 East 35 Street, New York, NY 10016. Reprinted with permission.

Between 1979 and 1982, the Soviet Union gave Nicaragua $150 million in military assistance and $50 million in economic assistance. The House *Democrats* have been quite candid about Soviet activities in Central America. The Majority Report of the House Select Committee on Intelligence asserts that the Salvadoran insurgency "depends for its lifeblood—arms, ammunition, financing, logistics, and command-and-control facilities—upon outside assistance from Nicaragua and Cuba. This Nicaraguan-Cuban contribution to the Salvadoran insurgency is longstanding. It began shortly after the overthrow of Somoza in July 1979. It has provided—by land, sea, and air—the great bulk of the military equipment and support received by the insurgents."

Thus, a marvelous turnabout has suddenly occurred, such that the factual situation in Central America is no longer in dispute. The cover stories of six months ago—that the Sandinistas and the guerrillas in El Salvador were pluralistic democrats, independent of Havana and Moscow—have been discarded. Thus, both the moderate Left and the far Left have changed their line of argument.

The new line runs as follows: Yes, Havana has received $4 billion in military aid from Moscow (and $28 billion in economic aid). Yes, Havana and Tripoli and Hanoi and Sofia and the PLO supply guns and bombs to Managua. Yes, Managua affords bases, supplies, and communication to the guerrillas in El Salvador. And, yes, the aim of all this international effort is to build Marxist states throughout Central America.

Marxism, So What?

But (yes, there's a *but*)—if Central America desires a Marxist political economy, so what? Marxist states are no threat to the United States. The proper national interest of the United States is to *support* Marxist revolution. The U.S. should support the creation of Marxist states—and then buy them off. Wean them from Moscow. Make Central America safe for national Communism. Let a thousand Titos bloom.

Thus do the real issues, under the pressure of open debate and indisputable real events, finally break into light. Proposed lines of action, then, come down to two: 1) the advance of Marxist states must be halted and reversed; 2) the emergence of Marxist states must be supported and bought off. Fight or appease.

The calculation among the Marxist powers today is that the United States will not fight for Central America. Resistance will be financial, political, and verbal; it will collapse on the field of battle. The next seven years will tell the tale. By 1990, Central America is likely to be Marxist or democratic. The longer the delay in military resistance on the field of battle, the more costly the battle will become.

Moralists are fond of saying that Christianity is a religion of peace. Historically, this has certainly not been true. Christianity has been a "fighting faith," notably so in the five centuries from the First Crusade until the Battle of Lepanto. (Otherwise, we would all be Moslems now and oil would probably lie still unused under the sands of Saudi Arabia.) It was so, also, under Luther, Calvin, and Cromwell. It was so in "the fighting 69th." It was so, after a decade of appeasement, in World War II. Christianity will always be a fighting faith. For it is realistic about sin and power. It is not a spiritualist faith but an incarnational faith, doing daily combat with Principalities and Powers.

What Christians must fight for in Central America is *not* the existing regimes. It is new and revolutionary regimes—regimes at once democratic and pluralist. José Napoleón Duarte of El Salvador knows what democracy really means: the possibility of electoral defeat. Unlike Fidel Castro and the Sandinistas' Daniel Ortega, he willingly faced the voters and accepted their rejection.

Communism Is Winning

"Communism is evil": A George McGovern or an Edward Kennedy would rather turn blue in the face than utter these three little words, though they do explain things like the Berlin Wall, the Cambodian holocaust, the Vietnamese boat people, and the preferences of the voters of El Salvador. Simplistic! Cold War rhetoric! McCarthyism! But true.

It is one of the terrible facts about human nature that the more successful an evil becomes, the more it destroys even our power to perceive it as evil. Everyone denounces Nazism and Fascism: They lost the war, and it costs nothing to recognize them as the horrors they were.

But communism has been winning, and renewing its assaults, so people make excuses for it and grant it diplomatic status and steer clear of conflict with it.

Joseph Sobran, *Conservative Digest*, June 1983.

The protection of human rights, in Central America or elsewhere, is not achieved by installing a new regime. It is achieved only by installing democratic institutions. Of the 160 nations of the world, the thirty or so with the highest rankings in respect for human rights are all functioning democracies, within which citizens govern themselves through regularly expressed consent. Tyrannies of non-democratic persuasion (whatever their ideology and propaganda) invariably abuse human rights.

So what is to be done? Marxism is not an evil because it installs

175

a socialist economy. If a nation wishes to thwart its own economic growth and permanently impoverish itself, that is its own business. ("If the Sahara were socialized, there would soon be a shortage of sand.") If the people want to wait in line for meat, eggs, and milk that is their own business.

Marxism Is Evil

Marxism is an evil because its foreign policy *cannot* be isolationist. Marxism is a quasi-religion. Its essence is a vision of power in history, power necessarily flowing toward the police and the military might of Marxist states. Marxist states do not, and cannot, believe in international laissez-faire. Believing Marxists acquire a moral obligation to carry Marxism, by force, to all the nations. To think of Marxism as a sort of extreme New Deal for peasants and workers is a bourgeois illusion. In Marxist states, the hard utopians always dominate the soft utopians. They take care to control three things: the secret police, the military, and the media.

Westerners, especially religious persons, find it difficult to take hard Marxists at their word. They think it moral to "trust" Marxists, to "love" them, and to "negotiate" with them "in good faith." But this is not morality. It is a colossal failure of moral imagination. This is the classic moral weakness of the children of light.

Biblical realists must prepare for war in Central America. Only such preparations will force Managua, Havana, and Moscow to grasp their own miscalculations about Christian realism. Faced with resolute military power, they will back down. They did so in the Cuban missile crisis in 1962. They will do so again. They pay attention, alas, only to power. It is our moral and our Christian responsibility to "dialogue" with them in the only language they understand.

The Role of Communism in Central America

President Reagan claimed that the Soviet Union is "the focus of evil in the modern world." He described US/Soviet relations as a struggle between good and evil. Many disagree with the President's analysis. One of these critics is a Harvard Law School professor, Harold J. Berman. Professor Berman argues that President Reagan "has confronted us with one of the profound questions of American history: what is the nature of evil, and what is the right way for America to combat it?"

The purpose of this exercise is to investigate the nature of the communist threat and the appropriate American response. Are the President's comments factual and helpful or are they possibly opinionated and potentially harmful? Do Professor Berman's comments direct attention to a real problem in America or distract the reader from what Mr. Reagan feels is the primary menace, Soviet evil and the worldwide threat it represents?

Instructions:

Part 1

Step 1.   Break into small discussion groups of four to six individuals. Each individual should read the two opposing viewpoints below.

Viewpoint One: Ronald Reagan

There is sin and evil in the world. And we are enjoined by Scripture and the Lord Jesus to oppose it with all our might. Our nation, too, has a legacy of evil with which it must deal. The glory of this land has been its capacity for transcending the moral evils of our past. . . .

The Soviet leaders have openly and publicly declared that the only morality they recognize is that which will further their cause, which is world revolution. . . .

Morality is entirely subordinate to the interests of class war. And everything is moral that is necessary for the annihilation of the old, exploiting social order and for uniting the proletariat. . . .

Yes, let us pray for the salvation of all of those who live in that totalitarian darkness—pray that they will discover the joy of knowing God. But until they do, let us be aware that while they preach the supremacy of the state, declare its omnipotence over individual man, and predict its eventual domination of all peoples on the Earth—*they* are the focus of evil in the modern world.

Presidential Documents, March 14, 1983.

Viewpoint Two: Harold Berman

His fallacy, and that of many Americans, is in the conception of the nature of evil. Early Christian theologians depicted the Devil as a fallen angel. He is by no means ineffectual, unintelligent, unattractive or even inhumane. What makes him the Devil, as Episcopal Bishop Richard Emrich once wrote, is not that he lacks virtues but that he is going in the wrong direction.

In the Bible the Devil offers Christ bread, power over the kingdoms of the world and miracles if Christ will worship him. Communism, as embodied in the Soviet system, offers its followers economic security, military power and sensational technological progress, all in return for one thing: absolute subservience to the high priests of these gods, the party leadership. . . .

In America's greatest novel, "Moby Dick," Melville warns against the self-righteousness that externalizes evil and tries to crush it by force. Captain Ahab, in wreaking vengeance on the White Whale, "the mono-maniac incarnation of. . .malicious agencies," destroys himself and his crew. Reagan's belief that Soviet communism is "the focus of evil in the modern world," and that the United States represents the forces of good evokes Jesus' description of the Pharisee who thanks God that "I am not as other men are, extortioners, unjust, adulterers, or even as the publican." Such self-righteousness cuts off virtually all possibility of negotiation and conciliation. But worse, in distracting us from the true nature of evil it leads to the same idolatry of material goods, military power and technological miracles that has tempted our adversary.

Newsweek, May 9, 1983.

Step 2.   After reading the two viewpoints, examine the statements below. Try to determine if each statement is a statement of fact or a statement of opinion. (For example, to say the United States was militarily involved in Vietnam is a statement of fact. But to say this involvement served US interests is a statement of opinion and may or may not be true.) As you examine each statement, try to reach a group consensus before going on to the next.

The following statements were made by President Ronald Reagan.

_____ 1. America is good. And if America ever ceases to be good, America will cease to be great.

_____ 2. I want you to know that this Administration is motivated by a political philosophy that sees the greatness of America. . .the institutions that foster and nourish values like concern for others and respect for the rule of law under God.

_____ 3. There is sin and evil in the world. And we are enjoined by the Lord Jesus to oppose it with all our might.

_____ 4. The Soviet leaders have openly and publicly declared that the only morality they recognize is that which will further their cause, which is world revolution.

_____ 5. The Soviet leaders. . .are the focus of evil in the modern world.

_____ 6. We want to see a world that lives in peace and freedom under the consent of the governed.

_____ 7. America remains the greatest force for peace anywhere in the world today.

_____ 8. It is America that encourages the trend toward democracy in Latin America.

_____ 9. The Communist agenda. . .is to exploit human suffering in Central America to strike at the heart of the Western Hemisphere. By preventing reform and instilling their own brand of totalitarianism, they can threaten freedom and weaken our national security.

_____ 10. For the past 3 years, under two presidents, the United States has been engaged in an effort to stop the advance of communism in Central America by doing what we do best—by supporting democracy.

Part 2

Step 1.   Each small group should write four statements which the group agrees are statements of fact. Write one statement on each of the following issues:

1. The role and responsibility of the USSR for world evil and international violence.
2. The role of the USSR in Central America.
3. How may the US best respond to Central American turmoil?
4. How does Central American unrest affect US national security?

Step 2.   Each group should share the conclusions it reached on both parts of this exercise with the other groups involved.

Periodical Bibliography

The following list of periodical articles deals with the subject matter of this chapter.

Commonweal

"Return to Central America," June 15, 1984.

Juan Corradi

"Nicaragua, Can It Find Its Own Way?" *Dissent*, Summer 1984.

Allan Dodds Frank

"The Real El Salvador," *Forbes*, March 29, 1982.

Joan Frawley

"The Idea of El Salvador in the United States," *Catholicism in Crisis*, June 1984.

Max Hugel

"Central America and Marxist Revolution," *Conservative Digest*, July 1983.

James Kelly, and others

"Starting a New Chapter," *Time*, June 11, 1984.

Robert Manning

"Dominoes May Fall If They Are Pushed," *The New York Times*, October 14, 1983.

Susanna McBee

"Why Distrust of U.S. Runs Deep," *U.S. News and World Report*, October 17, 1983.

Jim McClure

"The Gathering Storm in Central America," *New Guard*, Summer 1983.

Sergio Ramirez Mercado

"On Nicaragua's Resolve," *World Policy Journal*, Spring 1984.

Ronald Reagan

Published address on Central America, *The New York Times*, May 10, 1984.

Ronald Reagan

"U.S. Interests in Central America," *Department of State Bulletin*, June 1984.

David Reed

"High Stakes in Central America," *Reader's Digest*, August 1983.

Tony Smith

"Learn to Talk Hawk," *The New York Times*, September 12, 1983.

Viron P. Vaky

"What Do We Want in Nicaragua," *The New York Times*, June 18, 1984.

Is Peace Possible in Central America?

"[American] intervention would be more or less forgiven if it led to real democratization."

Military Action Can Bring Peace

Robert Wesson

Robert Wesson is a senior research fellow at Stanford University's Hoover Institution and a professor of political science at the University of California, Santa Barbara. His degrees include an M.A. from the Fletcher School of Law and diplomacy and a Ph.D. from Columbia University. Mr. Wesson is the author of *The Imperial Order* and *State Systems* and contributes numerous articles to *The New York Times* and *The Los Angeles Times*. In the following viewpoint, he explains how US military intervention can lead to a truly democratic order in Central America.

As you read, consider the following questions:

1. According to Mr. Wesson, what effect would American military intervention have upon the Soviet Union?
2. Does the author believe that American intervention would have any negative effects. If so, what would they be?
3. According to the author, what should be the ultimate aim of American military intervention?

Robert Wesson, "A Military Solution in Central America Can Work, If?" *Christian Science Monitor*, August 30, 1983. Reprinted with permission of the author.

In view of the military activities the administration has undertaken in Central America. . .it would be appropriate to consider likely consequences of intervention against the Sandinista government of Nicaragua. First, of course, would be the substitution of that government by one more friendly to the United States. There might be difficulties, because the anti-Sandinistas are totally divided and various leaders would rush forward to claim the succession. But this would hardly be a problem compared to dealing with the commanders now in Managua.

The Salvadorean guerrilla war would probably be concluded victoriously without having to engage US forces. Seeing their cause hopeless and lacking a Nicaraguan base, the Cubans and Soviets would end moral, financial, and material support for the guerrillas. El Salvador could return to normalcy, and Washington could happily forget about it.

For good or ill, rightist and military governments in Latin America would be encouraged, and the entire region might well be stabilized for a time. The Soviet Union might be discouraged from further probes in this hemisphere.

The Negative Side

It is possible, however, that the Soviet Union might count it a plus to have provoked the US into engaging its forces and attention in Central America instead of the Near East or Eastern Europe. There are other negative aspects to the situation. Many Europeans, confused by the issues, would see little difference between the American action and Soviet intervention to keep satellites in line, and opposition to deployment of missiles in Western Europe and to NATO in general would probably increase.

Latin Americans would nearly all believe that the US action was taken on behalf of US commercial interests and multinational corporations. The Sandinistas, removed from power, would be saved in history, raised from a group of dogmatists incapable of managing a country to heroes of the anti-Yankee cause. It would be taken as adequate proof that the US will put down, by force if necessary, a people's government in Latin America—the worst in the series from Guatemala in 1954 through Chile in 1973.

Overall, it could be fairly disastrous for the American reputation as a law-abiding, pacific, democratic power. Democratic powers are not supposed to engage in aggressive actions, even under a good deal of provocation, as the Eisenhower administration emphasized in castigating Britain and France for the Suez foray of 1956.

The damage to the American image would be especially severe

if it used the opportunity to restore status quo ante, that is, to restore and guarantee the rightist, more or less dictatorial forces. In that case, the old troubles would certainly recur, although not until long after the next election; and the Marxists would be believed when they say, "We told you so; capitalism shows its claws," and proclaim the necessity of revolution.

The Positive Side

On the other hand, damage to the American image could be compensated, and the intervention would be more or less forgiven, if it led to real democratization. This does not mean the holding of elections, which have usually been meaningless in Central America, but the remaking of Central American societies.

Decisive Action Needed

Given the present course of rhetorical proposals, we are headed for another Vietnam—a limited war that will end in another disaster—either in the eventual sacrifice of many American soldiers when the token aid escalations prove to be insufficient, or in the lives and loss of freedom of millions of our Latin American friends if the present paralysis over using our own military forces continues. $60 million or $600 million per year will never overcome the enemy unless we have the will to drive the entire threat out of this hemisphere. I am also convinced, that the more firm our resolve, and the more dramatic our offensive posture, the less costly the final outcome will be.

Joel M. Skousen, *Conservative Digest*, June 1983.

This can be done. The social order of Japan and West Germany was remade by the American occupation after World War II. The problem in Central America is more difficult but not impossible. First, it would be necessary to eliminate the old privileged classes. In Nicaragua, this has been done by the Sandinistas, but a host of people would clamor to get back their old properties and status. Despite all desires to be nice to our follies, they must be denied; after all, their shortsightedness had a lot to do with causing the trouble in the first place.

Likewise in El Salvador, democratization requires removal of the military and civilian oligarchs. In any case, they have never been friends, only clients willing to accept aid. There should also be thorough land reform, preferably eliminating all properties dependent on many hired hands. This would be costly in terms of production for some years, but individual farming would ultimately be more productive and would provide a sound basis for a democratic system.

In addition, education should make it possible for anyone to rise to any position; health services should be established to improve the capacities of the poor, especially children; there should be real taxes on income and wealth; an independent press should be fostered, as should free trade unions; local self-government should be set up; and so forth. This would require considerable expenditure and perhaps a decade of application, but it is perfectly feasible if there is sufficient will to do it.

In sum, it behooves the administration, as it moves in the direction of military intervention, to consider carefully how it can make the US not ashamed of its actions (however excusable on national security grounds) but proud of creating truly democratic societies, not only for the benefit of Central Americans but as an example for the rest of Latin America and the third world.

"The United States can set a tone and an atmosphere in Central America which is conducive to. . .encouraging the opportunity for diplomatic dialogue."

Diplomatic Action Can Bring Peace

James Hickey

James Hickey is the Archbishop of Washington, D.C. and chancellor of the Catholic University of America. In 1983, he gave testimony to the National Commission on US Policy in Central America, the bi-partisan committee known as the Kissinger Commission. He testified on behalf of the US Catholic Conference. In the following viewpoint, taken from that testimony, Archibishop Hickey outlines the steps the US should take for achieving a diplomatic solution to the Central American conflict.

As you read, consider the following questions:

1. What are the author's two concerns regarding current US involvement in Central America?
2. According to the author, what are some of the basic criteria for evaluating present and future US policies in Central America?
3. What does the author believe should be the goals of US policy?

James Hickey, in testimony before the National Commission on US Policy in Central America, 1983.

The American Catholic bishops come to this discussion with several perspectives. As Americans, we want to see our vital national interests protected and our government's policies reflect our national values and ideals.

As citizens we want U.S. policies to help bring about greater justice, democracy and stability in this hemisphere and to limit communist influence in the region. . . .

For that reason and on that basis, we welcome this opportunity to share our deep concerns about the future course of U.S. policy and activity. We fear that future U.S. policy may be based on a number of misconceptions regarding the basic issues and choices in Central America.

Roots of the Conflict

One concern is that the conflict in Central America is too often seen as primarily a geopolitical battle—a struggle between East and West, between the United States and the Soviet Union. We have repeatedly pointed out that long before there was outside intervention there was a legitimate struggle in El Salvador and other parts of the region for social, political and economic justice. The conflict has been over land, wages, the right to organize, and the issue of political participation. To ignore this long struggle of people for justice, dignity and freedom is fundamentally to misunderstand the nature of the conflict today in Central America.

Because the conflicts in Central America are fundamentally rooted in questions of social injustice and the persistent denial of basic human rights for large sectors of the population, the USCC has always opposed interpretations of the Salvadoran and Central American conflict which place primary emphasis on the superpower or East-West rivalry. This is not to ignore the international implications and dimensions of the conflict. Nor to deny the willingness of outside actors such as the Soviet Union to take full advantage of the crisis. But we urge the commission to reject the notion that the geopolitical struggle is at the core of the problem in Central America.

The Search for a Military Solution

A second concern is the continuing pursuit of a military solution for Central America. U.S. statements move back and forth on this question, but our actions speak more clearly—U.S. policy still has hopes that military force can solve the problems.

In El Salvador victory by either side, which could only mean abject surrender and bitter defeat for a large number of Salvadorans on one side or the other, would not serve the interest of either El Salvador or the United States. A society divided into victors and vanquished is unlikely to result in either stable peace or justice. Likewise, if the U.S.-backed "contras" were to somehow topple the government of the Sandinistas, do U.S. policymakers really believe that would bring peace and stability to Nicaragua or the region? We hope the commission will make clear that a continuing military struggle in an already devastated region is not in our interests or Central America's. . . .

A Diplomatic Solution

The US, Soviet Union, Cuba, and all other governments of the region could pledge not to intervene or interfere in the internal affairs of other nations of the area, provided others also fulfill their commitments.

Some have criticized this proposal as suggesting a role for the Soviet Union in dealing with hemispheric problems. But the hard fact is—as we have been told repeatedly by the President—that the Soviet Union *is* playing a role and is supplying help and support in Cuba, Nicaragua, and elsewhere. It is ironic that some of those most insistent that the Soviet Union is behind much of the current Central American turmoil reject the suggestion that the US discuss their involvement with them to see if there is maybe a mutually agreeable basis for bringing the fighting to an end. By the same token, since Cuba is clearly playing a significant part in the military struggle, the Contadora countries might undertake to examine the possibility of some understanding with Cuba to resolve the conflict.

Sol Linowitz, from testimony before a House subcommittee on the report issued by the Inter-American Dialogue, a forum of 48 prominent hemisphere and North American leaders.

When U.S. policymakers talk about the dangers of outside interference in Central America, they refer to the Soviet Union and its proxies. When Central Americans talk about outside interference they are talking about the Soviets to be sure, but they are also talking about the United States. There is no need to recite the sad history of U.S. intervention in the region, a living memory for the people and leaders of Central America. The present and past experience of intervention has led to the unified opposition by the Latin American hierarchies to all outside intervention without exception. By outside intervention they do not refer to the efforts of other Latin American states to facilitate political dialogue; such efforts the bishops specifically endorse.

Rather, the unacceptable interference is that of the "foreign powers," essentially the Soviet Union and the United States. Latin America does not expect, nor desire, the United States simply to forfeit any active role in the Latin American quest for peace and development. Still less do they welcome expanded Soviet influence in any area of the hemisphere. What they oppose now more strongly than ever in the past, is in the words of the Central American bishops, "the meddling of foreign powers who come to support those in the countries who fit their own interests which are generally far from, even opposed to, those of the great majority.". . .

Human Rights

One inconsistent aspect of the debate over Central America is the use of human rights criteria for tactical advantage or propaganda points rather than as a steady and consistent benchmark for governments in the region and our relationships with them. Selective application of human rights standards depending on our ideological preferences erodes our credibility both at home and abroad. Human rights are being violated throughout the region.

The people of Central America are assaulted by death squads, arbitrary imprisonment, uninvestigated murders, harassment of land reform efforts, restrictions on free union activity, interference in education and journalism, and other threats to life and freedom. While life itself is threatened in some parts of the region, human freedom and social justice are too often violated by powerful interests and governments across Central America. We need a consistent policy which sees human rights as a principal focus of U.S. concern, not as debater's points in our policy discussions. We hope this commission will make respect for human rights a fundamental criterion for U.S. policy for all nations in the region.

In dealing with these concerns, we need a clear vision of our goals and a way to judge which policies hold the best chance of achieving them. Permit me to suggest some basic criteria for evaluating both present and future policies:

—Do they move the parties toward diplomatic rather than military options, toward ceasefire, dialogue and negotiations? Toward free and open elections where all can participate without the threat of violence or coercion?

—Do they increase respect for human rights and basic freedoms? Do they make respect for human rights a consistent standard for governments in the region?

—Do they address basic issues of social justice, genuine land reform, broad participation in development and economic justice? Do they in fact offer hope of a better life for the poor and dispossessed in the region?

—Do they build the capacity of people and their governments in the region to deal with their own problems? Do they promote self-determination and self-sufficiency?

—Do they respect and respond to the cultural, ethical and religious values of the people of Central America or impose answers from a distance?

—Do they respect and support the positive role of non-governmental and local institutions (churches, small business, trade unions, cooperatives, etc.)?

—Do they strengthen the hand of moderate and democratic forces or, by further polarization, help the extremes of both right and left? Do they combat communism by offering alternatives to Marxism as vehicles for needed reform?

—Do they support effective civilian control of the military, the rule of law and an effective criminal justice system? . . .

US Dismisses Negotiations

There is, in fact, another and reasonable solution to the Central America imbroglio: negotiations. In theory, the Reagan administration is committed to "dialogue and negotiations." Almost no close observers have any confidence that the administration's notion of negotiations amounts to much more than arranging for the Salvadoran insurgents' surrender and the Sandinistas' exit from power. President Reagan has declared the region a "vital interest" in terms which hardly allow the survival of anything but regimes reliably in the American orbit. As Undersecretary of Defense Fred Ikle put it, "We do not seek a military stalemate. We seek victory for the forces of democracy." The U.S. has repeatedly undercut or dismissed efforts at negotiations; the last round of Sandinista gestures was met with heightened American demands.

Commonweal, May 4, 1984.

The first requirement for future U.S. policy in Central America is to change the basic thrust of present policy and stop the drift toward a regional war in Central America. Among our goals in Central America should be a group of states developing and maturing under viable political systems, enjoying good relations with one another and with us. Therefore, our policy should foster regional stability through efforts which encourage the individual nations to reach an accommodation with one another and settle their differences without outside intervention or arms.

In Central America there are some tasks the United States is well-suited to fulfill and other tasks which we should leave to other actors. I believe the United States can set a tone and an atmosphere in Central America which is conducive to diminishing the military elements of the struggle and encouraging the opportunity for diplomatic dialogue. . . .

A second essential choice for the future is the acceptance, and more than that, the welcoming of dramatic social change to achieve social justice and human rights in the region. We need to define U.S. interest in a way which recognizes and supports substantial political and economic change in countries needing both. If we fail to define our interests to accommodate change, we are fated to oppose it. This will place the United States in opposition to the majority of the people in a region which cries out for change. . . .We must support genuine land reform and other efforts to eliminate the enormous inequities in the region. . . .

In the past, U.S. policy toward Central America has too often been seen as defending the status quo and authoritarian regimes. Future policies cannot ask people to choose between the status quo and revolutionary violence, between continued injustice and Marxism. U.S. policy, given our history and traditional values, should stand as a beacon of hope, a force for justice and a defender of human rights.

"Many people in the region. . .have known only one danger against their national integrity, and that has been the American danger."

The US Endangers Peace in Central America

Carlos Fuentes

Carlos Fuentes is a Mexican writer, editor, and diplomat. He is the former Mexican Ambassador to France and was head of the department of cultural relations in the Mexican Ministry of Foreign Affairs. He is famous for his fiction, much of which is a synthesis of reality and fantasy. His novels include *Terra Nostra, The Death of Artemio Cruz,* and *Aqua Quemada.* In the following viewpoint, Mr. Fuentes claims that US policy in Central America has contributed to the ever-growing tensions in that region.

As you read, consider the following questions:

1. What does the word "Sandinismo" mean?
2. According to the author, what have the current governments of Cuba and Nicaragua done for their people?
3. What does the author write about US involvement in El Salvador; Nicaragua; Honduras; Costa Rica; and Guatemala?

As a Mexican, I am particularly concerned about United States policy in Central America, since it will inevitably hurt or help my country. Mexico is living through the most acute economic crisis since the revolution. That the crisis is not yet political is due to the revolution itself. Whatever the failings of the Mexican experience since 1910 (and God knows they are many and large), we have managed to attain a remarkable stability and to avoid the extremes of anarchy or repression. This is so because the revolution created institutions that then furthered stability.

What we see in Central America, from our Mexican experience, is the absence or weakness of political institutions, the resistance of the prevailing structures to reform, and the desperation of many groups suffering under long-standing injustice. . . .

What does "Sandinismo" mean to many of these humiliated peoples? It means that you no longer take orders from the United States ambassador. It means that you are no longer a United States base. It is as simple as that. The problem for many Latin Americans is not that Nicaragua might become a Soviet base. The invasions against Guatemala in 1954 and against Cuba in 1961 were launched from Somoza's Nicaragua. Many people in the region are impervious to thoughts about Soviet danger because they have known only one danger against their national integrity, and that has been the American danger. . . .

Irony of US Influence

The perception of the United States by Latin Americans as the paramount regional power in terms comparable to the perception of the Soviet Union by the people of Eastern Europe should not be underestimated. Many defects and errors of a revolutionary regime are pardoned or overlooked by the majority of its people because they feel that the new government has finally lifted the weight of American hegemony. Therefore, attacks by the United States serve only to strengthen the government Washington would like to see overthrown. The same would be true, *mutatis mutandis*, if a right-wing, militantly Catholic, anti-Semitic, and fascistic government managed to come to power in Poland. Its policies would generally be accepted if at the same time such a neo-Pilsudskian government broke Polish subservience to the U.S.S.R.

It follows that a revolutionary regime, on the basis of its anti-American posture, can mobilize the people for its internal radical goals. Again, many Latin Americans feel that, whatever their shortcomings, the regimes in Cuba and Nicaragua have done what no previous governments in those countries were capable of doing: mobilizing the people; finding solutions to problems of literacy, health, nutrition, and life expectancy; and

I PLEDGE A BILLION TO THE FLAG

OF THE RIGHT WING GOVERNMENT OF EL SALVADOR

AND TO THE DEATH SQUADS FOR WHICH IT STANDS

ONE NATION, UNDERFED...

INDEFENSIBLE

WITH M-16S AND HOWITZERS FOR ALL...

PETERS, Dayton Daily News

Reprinted by permission of United Features Syndicate.

at the same time imposing, at a high price, a politics of equality. . . .These are seen as enormous achievements in the light of a history dominated by privilege, extreme inequality, and callousness toward the needs of the majority. The association of the word "democracy" with governments incapable of coming to grips with these problems or indeed bent on maintaining the status quo only furthers the derogatory comparisons.

Yet a revolution that does not face, sooner or later, its duties to the democratic dimension runs the danger of sacrificing even its best material achievements. As a writer I am of course concerned by the problems of political freedom, human rights, and intellectual liberties in revolutionary societies. My concern is nuanced by the experience of my own country. Mexico has not achieved a fully democratic polity, although it has made gigantic strides toward nationhood while keeping open the channels of intellectual diversity. As I see the new revolutions coming, my preoccupation is perhaps not the central preoccupation of countries that have never practiced true democracy. But the question

195

remains. The people now read. The children do not die. What will they read? What kind of political beings shall they grow up to be?

National Mobilization

One answer lies in the very mobilization I have referred to. The people of Central America have never been asked to move, but to abide. In Nicaragua, as in Mexico in the Twenties and Thirties, a liberation from traditional servitudes has occurred; the people are participating in myriad aspects of the national life from which they were historically excluded. They have been handed arms. This also happened in Mexico under Cárdenas. An irreversible momentum is thus gained, and its goal is greater freedom, even beyond the regime's expectations. This momentum is not something instantaneous. It is a response to situations that began with Columbus.

It is just this dynamism that first provokes enthusiasm and then serious misgivings as the price of national mobilization rises. Then a renewed solidarity appears as the United States responds with excessive alarm to different aspects of the new situation. A point is reached when we would all like to see the revolutions enter a stage in which anti-Americanism is not defined negatively, but as positive independence. Mexico has reached this stage. Cuba and Nicaragua have not. The United States perhaps must pay in patience for the many decades of its political and economic abuse of Central America and weather the rhetoric by which small but proud nations sublimate old and often justified animosities. After all, Anastasio Somoza and his brood were not put in power by Joseph Stalin. . . .

But what about the alleged Cuban and Nicaraguan interventions in other Central American countries? What about the strength of the Nicaraguan army? What about the fear of Nicaraguan aggression against its neighbors? At this stage of the game, all these questions have spectral twins. What about United States intervention in El Salvador and Honduras? What about the strength of American naval flotillas on both shores of Nicaragua? What about the fear of American aggression, through proxies, against Nicaragua? Indeed, what about the aggression against stability and national integrity in Costa Rica and Panama? . . .

Central American States

El Salvador. This conflict was born and bred in the political history of that unfortunate nation. Cuba and Nicaragua could well sink into the sea, and the U.S.S.R. contract to medieval Novgorod: the local, bitter struggle in El Salvador would continue.

196

Only the direct involvement of American armed forces can defeat the guerrillas (momentarily: wait five, ten, or twenty years . . .). This is an unlikely event. Therefore the Salvadoran army does not want victory. That would mean the end of American aid. It does not want successful negotiations for the same reason. In effect, the United States has become the captive of the Salvadoran military, not the other way around. In El Salvador, negotiations do not signify "power sharing." They simply signify that the army shall be brought under some sort of control so that truly free elections can take place. Please recall that the opposition in El Salvador (and in Guatemala) has been and continues to be decimated by death squads whenever its members have tried to join the political process. Controlling the army should be the central theme of negotiations in El Salvador. In the course of such an *apertura*, an opportunity might conceivably arise to reconstitute a semblance of the left-center alliance that democratically won the elections in 1972 and was promptly thwarted from taking power by the military. Such an opportunity should now be seized if it appears.

Policy of Destabilization

The United States has openly admitted its policy of destabilization against the Sandinista government of Nicaragua, supplying counseling, training and weapons to the members of the former National Guard of the late dictator of that country. Several regimes that receive support and help from the United States, violate every type of human rights and represent a dominating oligarchy that does not serve in any way the interests of the majority of the people, and are repressive and criminal dictatorships.

Esdras A. Rodriguez, *engage/social action*, December 1983.

Nicaragua. What we fear in Mexico is that the consequences of a military action there have not been truly thought out. Nicaragua is not Guatemala in 1954 or Chile in 1973: the government in Managua has an armed populace behind it. The overthrow of the government would only take it to the *maquis*. They are perfectly prepared to offer long-term resistance. Sandino managed to pin the Marines down in Nicaragua for six years. He had only rifles and machetes. The tide this time would engulf the country in one of the most bitter civil wars this continent has known. The contras back in Managua would stage a bloodbath and restore the old tyranny: what would prevent it? The wild cards of Pastora and Robelo coming from the south would add to the confusion. The quick fix would turn out to be a prolonged agony.

Honduras. We see this country becoming an American base and liquidating its modest political gains under outright military takeover. Already, Gen. Gustavo Alvarez Martínez is considered the man who gives the orders, not President Suazo Córdova. The civilian government withers, the Salvadoran collusion of a corrupt military and a corrupt oligarchy takes over, the military starts milking the United States, and the stage is set for a new El Salvador as the center-left becomes marginal and desperate.

Costa Rica. This country does not want to become a U.S. base. San José is already the Beirut of Central America, with all the contending factions of the region represented there. This tinderbox will explode if Costa Rica cannot maintain sovereignty over its borders under the pressure of U.S.-backed contras.

Guatemala. This country offers the best example of why the "quick fix" does not work. The elected moderate-left government of Jácobo Arbenz, itself the product of the Guatemalan revolution of 1944, was overthrown in 1954 by an invasion led by Col. Carlos Castillo Armas and avowedly financed and directed by the CIA and the American ambassador in Guatemala City. Guatemala has known nothing but civil strife, repression, and economic distress during the past thirty years. The fugitives from a policy akin to genocide press on the Mexican border and spill over. Nothing was gained by intervention. Three decades were lost. A democratic Guatemala would have been to everybody's benefit. . . .

An Alternative

There is a danger that in order to arrest a debatable Soviet influence in Central America, the United States would first alienate, destabilize, corrupt, and build up the future problems of the region, from Mexico to Panama. It would probably end up sacrificing lives: American and Latin American. The U.S. would gain nothing from giving in to the ambitions of the military in Central America. Neither democracy nor social progress is to be had in this way.

Peace through negotiations is the only real, politically enduring, and politically self-interested solution. There are dangers and there are costs. But these are infinitely lower than those assured by the recourse to war.

Throughout the region, including Mexico, Colombia, and Venezuela, young people are talking of forming brigades to join the Sandinistas in case of outright conflict. These brigades would catch (are catching) the imagination of many unemployed youths. There would be death counts of Mexican, Colombian, and Venezuelan boys on Mexico City, Bogotá, and Caracas TV.

Peace through negotiations would enhance the standing of the United States in the nations committed to the negotiating pro-

cess: Mexico, Venezuela, Colombia, and Panama. These governments are serving your interests better than you serve them
yourself. They are not being supported in their efforts by the administration in Washington. Gunboat diplomacy is felt as a
danger not only in Managua, but in all four Contadora capitals.
The issues for negotiation have been spelled out clearly and
tacitly approved by all concerned, except the United States.
These issues include: no Soviet bases or armed capabilities in
Central America; border patrols; no passage of arms; no foreign
military advisers; progressive demilitarization; strict respect for
the internal processes of each nation.

The success of negotiations would isolate the Soviet Union
from the process of change in Central America and bring in the
plural forces of Western Europe, Japan, and the multilateral
organizations. I would not go as far as to suggest that the United
States, in the name of its own origins, should embrace the
revolutionary movements in Latin America and love them to
death. But since the United States obviously cannot influence
the status quo, why doesn't it attempt to influence change. . .for
a change?

4

VIEWPOINT

"There is. . .no evidence that the Sandinistas are taking any of the essential measures which. . .could help being about. . .a viable and lasting peace."

Nicaragua Endangers Peace in Central America

Langhorne A. Motley

Langhorne A. Motley is the assistant secretary for Inter-American Affairs and former Ambassador to Brazil. The son of an American oil executive, he was born and grew up in Rio de Janeiro. He graduated from Citadel military school in Charleston, S.C. and served with the Air Force in Panama and Alaska. In the following viewpoint, Mr. Motley claims that the Sandinista government of Nicaragua has thwarted all geniune efforts aimed at a peaceful resolution of the Central American question.

As you read, consider the following questions:

1. What nations are part of the Contadora group?
2. What were the terms of the four draft treaties based on the Ortega proposals?
3. Does the author feel that Nicaraguan peace proposals are substantive or merely empty rhetoric? Explain your answer.

Langhorne A. Motley, in an address before the Foreign Policy Association in New York on January 19, 1984.

There's nothing easy about the situation in Central America. The issues are so complex and the situation changing so rapidly that everyone keeps looking for "signals" of what is happening—and what will happen next.

The signals today, as usual, are mixed. I want to talk very specifically about one kind of signal coming up from Central America: the signals which tell us on the one hand that peace is possible there and the ones that say the opposite. But before I even begin, remember that nations, like people, are capable of sending false signals—of making paper commitments that have no meaning.

With that in mind, let's look at some interesting signals.

• In January 1983, Colombia, Mexico, Panama, and Venezuela met on the island of Contadora to consider ways to prevent a widening conflict. After a slow beginning for what is now known as the Contadora process, all five Central American nations agreed in September to a document of objectives—21 in all—to serve as a basis for a comprehensive regional peace treaty. . . .

• In El Salvador, meanwhile, the fighting continued. But last year a large-scale amnesty was approved by the Constituent Assembly and effectively and humanely implemented. More than 1,000 guerrillas and camp followers came in from the cold. Two meetings took place between the Peace Commission and the guerrilla representatives. That dialogue was interrupted when the guerrillas refused even to discuss participating in the direct popular elections for president. . .But the Salvadoran Government has carefully left the door open to renewed contacts.

• In Nicaragua, the Sandinistas gradually softened the tone of their statements. They agreed formally to the 21 objectives of the Contadora process—objectives that include democratization, arms control, an end to support for subversion, and gradual withdrawal of foreign military and security advisers. In November, the Sandinistas signaled they were reducing their ties to Cuba and to the Salvadoran guerrillas. They also initiated a dialogue with some of their internal opposition—although they have not yet responded to a call from all major anti-Sandinista forces to implement their 1979 commitments to the Organization of American States (OAS) and allow all political elements to compete for power in free and genuinely fair elections.

Where Does Nicaragua Really Stand?

What does all this mean? Is there finally some reason to hope that Central America is on a course toward peace? Or are all these signals examples of the dashed hopes and propaganda that plague Central America? What is the evidence?

I'M HERE TO PROTECT NICARAGUA FROM THE SOMOCISTAS... THE PEOPLE DO NOT WANT ANOTHER DICTATORSHIP!

Let me start by reviewing the record with regard to Nicaragua. When in 1979 the Sandinistas formally pledged to the OAS to establish a democratic, pluralistic, and nonaligned regime, the United States took a leading role in the international effort to assist Nicaragua. In the first 21 months after the fall of Somoza, we authorized $117.2 million in economic assistance. Despite many problems, the Carter Administration suspended aid disbursements only after it became clear that the Sandinistas were supporting the guerrillas in El Salvador.

In October 1980 under President Carter, then again in August 1981 and April 1982 under the Reagan Administration, the United States sought to persuade Nicaragua to renounce its support of the guerrilla insurgency in El Salvador. The Nicaraguans did not respond to our concerns. In October 1982 in San Jose, Costa Rica, eight democratically elected governments made fair and balanced proposals for a regional peace. Nicaragua refused even to receive the Costa Rican Foreign Minister as emissary of this group.

The sources of Nicaragua's intransigence were clear. Internally, the Sandinista leaders had succeeded in removing from influence everyone who disagreed with them. They had built an army four times the size of Somoza's notorious National Guard. And they had developed close military ties to Cuba and the Soviet Union, which included thousands of advisers and a sophisticated joint effort to destabilize El Salvador and other neighboring governments.

The regime in Managua was so arrogantly confident in its ability to impose its will that it refused to listen to either its internal opposition or its neighbors. A former member of that regime, Arturo Cruz, put Nicaragua's situation in a nutshell in the summer 1983 issue of *Foreign Affairs*:

> There is . . . an element of self-destruction in the present conduct of the Revolution. Certain Sandinista revolutionary leaders' rejection of pragmatism is puzzling. The allegiance to an internationalist ideology . . . at the expense of the basic interests of the nation-state of Nicaragua, is unacceptable.

Then on the fourth anniversary of the Sandinista revolution, Junta Coordinator Daniel Ortega offered a six-point peace proposal. The proposal was one sided. It would, for example, have cut off all assistance to the Government of El Salvador while leaving Cuban and Soviet assistance to the Government of Nicaragua wholly unencumbered. It said nothing about democratization, foreign military advisers, or verification. But for the first time the Sandinistas accepted a multilateral dialogue and hinted at a willingness to suspend their support for the Salvadoran guerrillas. That much was encouraging, and we said so.

Costa Rica, El Salvador, Guatemala, and Honduras quickly seized the initiative. They put forward an eight-point proposal—the "Bases for Peace." Meeting in Panama under Contadora auspices, Nicaragua joined them in agreeing to the 21 objectives I mentioned earlier. The "Document of Objectives" called for the establishment of democratic systems of government; for the reduction of current inventories of arms and military personnel; for the proscription of foreign military bases; for the reduction and eventual elimination of foreign military advisers and troops; for an end to support for subversion; and for adequate means of verification and control. There were, and are, objectives on which a single, comprehensive, regional treaty could be based.

A Change of Policy

This agreement was important progress. But what was Nicaragua's next step?

On October 20, 1983—that is, just weeks after apparently accepting the 21 objectives—Nicaragua presented four draft treaties based on the Ortega proposals. These drafts:

• Disregarded the objective of restoring military balance among states of the region;

- Sought again to delegitimize the elected Government of El Salvador by treating it as simply one of two belligerent parties;
- Ignored the Contadora objective to establish democratic institutions; and
- Made no serious proposal for verification and control.

In reverting to its own partial agenda and presenting it at the United Nations, Nicaragua undercut the 21 objectives of Contadora, both procedurally and substantively. Instead of acting to build confidence that it was genuinely seeking accommodation, Nicaragua strengthened the arguments of those who saw its proposals as a renewed campaign of deception designed to *avoid* real accommodation. I repeat: In the guise of "negotiating," Nicaragua was *rejecting* accommodation.

Exporters of Revolution

What the Sandinistas have done to Nicaragua is a tragedy. But we Americans must understand and come to grips with the fact that the Sandinistas are not content to brutalize their own land. They seek to export their terror to every other country in the region. I ask you to listen closely to the following quotation: "We have the brilliant revolutionary example in Nicaragua. . .The struggle in El Salvador is very advanced: The same in Guatemala, and Honduras is developing quickly. . .very soon Central America will be one revolutionary entity." That statement was made by a Salvadoran guerrilla leader.

President Ronald Reagan, from an address delivered on May 9, 1984.

Then, in November, word began to spread that Nicaragua was reducing the Cuban presence; that it was asking the Salvadoran FMLN/FDR [Farabundo Marti National Liberation Front/Revolutionary Democratic Front] to leave Managua; and that a new dialogue with the church and internal opposition was beginning. In December, Nicaragua proposed a freeze on arms imports and the reciprocal withdrawal of foreign military advisers.

These signals suggested that Nicaragua recognized it would have to respond to the concerns expressed by its democratic opposition and by its neighbors in Central America.

The United States welcomed these signals. Secretary Shultz said so publicly. And, you may be confident, we have been exploring them thoroughly in our private diplomacy.

But the Secretary also said that what matters is the reality behind the rhetoric. Look at the evidence:

- Nicaragua claimed it was reducing the Cuban presence. But, as Interior Minister Borge himself admitted publicly, only normal, year-end rotations of teachers were involved. We have seen no evidence that any of Cuba's 2,000 military and security advisers have left Nicaragua. And while they, not teachers, are the main source of concern, we learned from Grenada that even construction workers can beat their shovels into AK-47s pretty quickly.

• Nicaragua had implied it was forcing the Salvadoran FMLN/FDR out of Managua. But although a few FDR leaders did leave Nicaragua, the FMLN's sophisticated command and control headquarters and infrastructure remain intact and operating in Nicaragua.

• Nicaragua claimed it was offering a generous amnesty to the Miskito Indians. Yet just before Christmas, another 1,200 Miskito men, women, and children chose to flee under hostile conditions into Honduras rather than suffer continued Sandinista repression.

In short, despite the rhetoric, there is still no *evidence* that the Sandinistas are taking any of the essential measures which, if actually implemented, could help bring about among the states of the region a viable and lasting peace.

To remove any possible ambiguity, let me say again what those measures are:

• The establishment of a genuinely democratic regime;
• A definitive end to Nicaragua's support for guerrilla insurgencies and terrorism;
• Severance of Nicaraguan military and security ties to Cuba and the Soviet bloc; and
• Reductions in Nicaraguan military strength to levels that would restore military balance between Nicaragua and its neighbors. . . .

The Hard Road Ahead

It is certainly too soon to conclude that an effective regional agreement can be achieved. The most difficult negotiations lie ahead. Substantive balance and effective verification and enforcement will be essential to move beyond a document of exhortation and good intentions. But it is encouraging that the Central Americans are pursuing their dialogue with persistence and realism. . . .

But no one should harbor any illusions that a treaty alone will resolve the crisis. Under the most optimistic of scenarios, we are a long way from an end to the crisis in Central America. Nicaragua has disproportionate military power controlled by a Marxist-Leninist minority operating without democratic checks.

"It should be possible to develop an aid strategy that will translate into meaningful programs of development for the advancement of all people."

A Marshall Plan Can Achieve Peace

M. C. Madhaven

M. C. Madhaven is a professor of economics at San Diego State University. He is the author of an article that deals with the distribution of wealth in Latin America. In the following viewpoint, Mr. Madhaven explains why he believes that a comprehensive foreign aid program will serve the cause of peace in Central America.

As you read, consider the following questions:

1. What was the late Senator Henry M. Jackson's attitude toward a "Marshall Plan" for Central America?
2. According to the author, are shifts in wealth taking place in Central America? What statistics does he quote to support his claims?
3. What are the author's feelings toward trade with Central American countries?

M.C. Madhaven, "What Would Latin Marshall Plan Do?" Originally published in the October 2, 1983 issue of the *San Diego Union*. Reprinted with permission.

The importance attached to Central American countries in U.S. foreign policy has been marked repeatedly by periods of neglect followed by periods of panic. Since the late 1970s, the United States has been in one of the latter periods, when long-term neglect is replaced by a belief that what happens in the region is of vital interest to this country.

Despite President Reagan's two-track policy of military threat to Marxist-dominated countries in the region and of economic and security assistance to friendly governments and groups, there is almost unanimity of opinion among experts that the long-term interest of the U.S. will be better served if our policies aim at improving the economic performance of these countries and at rectifying historical patterns of social injustice.

"Security assistance should be an adjunct to our Central American policy, not its foundation. We'd better face it, the shield will crumble unless we address the serious social and economic injustices in the region," said the late Sen. Henry M. Jackson, D-Wash., as he proposed a bipartisan commission to study an effort of Marshall Plan proportions to deal with the problem of security and economic development of the Central American countries. . . .

Great Sacrifices

Are the American people ready to accept the sacrifices an effort of these proportions would require at this time? Probably not, particularly when they are not sure about the assistance reaching the masses in Central American countries. The selling of a Marshall Plan-type program for Central America will not be easy, but it may be possible. With the experience gained in our aid relationship to date, it should be possible to develop an aid strategy that will translate into meaningful programs of development for the advancement of all people—including the poor and downtrodden, who so far have been excluded from enjoying the benefits of progress.

Significant economic growth in these countries in the last 20 years, notably in Costa Rica, does not seem to have contributed to reduction of the concentration of wealth and income in small segments of the population. The income gap between the rich and the poor seems to have widened rather than narrowed. The poor have become poorer, the rich richer. Excessive population growth has played an important role in widening the income gap. Per capita income of the upper 5 percent of households in a country could be as high as 15 times the median income of that country, in contrast to only five times in the U.S.

However, other measures of growth, in general, indicate an improvement in the quality of life in Central America. An average person has more to eat now than he had 20 years ago, even though per capita calorie consumption is still 6 to 8 percent less in El Salvador, Guatemala and Honduras than what is considered necessary. Education opportunities have improved, but still 40 to 50 percent of the people in El Salvador, Guatemala and Honduras don't know how to read and write. People have greater access to safe water now than before. Birth rates have declined, but have been more than offset by the decline in death rates in all but Costa Rica, where a dramatic decline in birth rates has helped the country to make a dent in population growth.

A Workable Plan

Accommodating all parties to the conflict will not be easy; it will tax the diplomatic skill and political will of everyone involved. But the alternative—untold years of bloodshed and poverty—would carry even greater human costs. Once the armed conflicts subside, equitable economic growth will foster the conditions in which free citizens can make a free choice of government. As Paul Hoffman, the Republican industrialist who administered the Marshall Plan, once remarked: "The best way to combat communism is with prosperity."

Edward F. Feighan, *The Christian Science Monitor,* August 3, 1983.

Another significant feature of the economies is a substantial increase in recent years in the share of gross national product devoted to military development in all but Costa Rica. Honduras spent over 8 percent of GNP in 1982 on non-economic activities, the highest in the region, followed by Nicaragua, El Salvador, Guatemala and Costa Rica. The growth in military expenditures was the sharpest in El Salvador, from 0.8 percent in 1972 to 4.1 percent in 1982. Combined with relatively low saving rates in many of them, high levels of expenditure on military development necessitated a considerable inflow of foreign capital to meet the growing investment needs of these countries.

The U.S. government and private sector have been the major sources of foreign funds. U.S. bilateral assistance to the Central American countries since World War II has amounted to over $3 billion and another $546 million is planned for fiscal 1984. Another $600 million was expended in the form of military aid. El Salvador is the largest recipient of economic as well as military aid, Guatemala the smallest amount of economic assistance and Costa Rica the smallest amount of military assistance.

El Salvador, Honduras and Guatemala received a lot more economic aid during the last three years than during the previous 18 years. Nicaragua has not received sizable amounts of aid since 1981, even though it has been getting $300,000 worth of agricultural commodity assistance through private, voluntary organizations. The economic aid requested by the administration will involve a sacrifice of $2.50 by every U.S. citizen, with another $0.50 for military assistance.

U.S. parent companies' claims on their subsidiaries in Central American countries were estimated in 1981 at $1,042 million, accounting for 2.7 percent of the direct investment position of all U.S. firms in Latin America or for less than one-half of one percent of U.S. firms' worldwide investment. U.S. firms are more deeply entrenched in Honduras, over $300 million; followed by Costa Rica and Guatemala, about $250 million each; El Salvador, over $100 million, and Nicaragua, less than $100 million.

Economically, strategic investment such as in mining plays a very minor role. Manufacturing and agriculture account for the principal U.S. investment in Central America.

Besides, the U.S. has been the most important trading partner of every Central American country, except Nicaragua, since 1982. And even though no longer the number one trading partner of Nicaragua, it exported goods worth about $118 million and imported goods valued at $87 million, leaving a trade balance favoring the U.S. However, U.S. trade with the Central America amounted to only one-half of one percent of U.S. foreign trade in 1982. No Central American country is a substantial exporter of strategic raw materials to the United States. Whatever minerals are being exported constitute very little of U.S. imports of those metals and even less of U.S. demand.

Lagging export growth and the high cost of borrowing have created acute debt servicing problems for Central America, most severe in Costa Rica with an estimated $4 billion in external debt. Every country in the region has signed agreements in recent months with the International Monetary Fund for new assistance, agreeing to follow policies they hope will put them on the road to improved performance.

This discussion suggests that U.S. economic interests in Central American countries are rather limited. But our policy in the past has clearly established that we have an important role to play in the region. Since it is no longer possible to impose the military solutions of the past without high political cost and excessive expenditure, political solutions for the present problems in the Central American region are *sine qua non* for U.S. aid diplomacy to be effective in achieving its foreign policy objectives.

In association with the Contadora Group, the U.S. should seek a Central American solution that will emphasize deescalation of the arms race in the region and establishment of a framework acceptable to contending forces within which future internal political changes can occur.

For this kind of an aid program to succeed, the U.S. must be prepared to commit technical manpower on a larger scale and deeply involve itself in the formulation and implementation of development programs (something the U.S. did not do in Europe) to benefit all people.

Table 1
Indices of development: Central American countries*

Indices	Costa Rica	El Salvador	Guat-emala	Hond-uras	Nicar-agua
1-a. Population (millions) 1983	2.4	5.1	7.9	4.1	3.0
1-b. Growth rate 1970-80	2.5	2.9	3.0	3.4	3.4
2. Life expectancy at birth in years (1981)	73	63	59	59	57
3-a. Per capita GNP in $ (1981)	1,430	650	1,140	600	860
3-b. Growth rate (1970-81)	6.7	2.4	7.1	8.3	-1.2
4. Per capita calorie consumption as % of requirement (1980)	116	99	93	96	99
5. Adult literacy rate (1980)	90	62	50	60	90
6. Percentage of population with access to safe water (1975)	77	53	40	46	70
7-a. Military expend-itures in millions of $ (1981 or 1982)	14	148	152	220	163
7-b. As a % of GNP	0.6	4.1	1.8	8.4	7.2
8. Domestic savings rate (1980 or 1981)	18	10	11	18	6
9. Domestic invest-ment rate (1980 or 1981)	28	12	17	24	24

*Note: Strictly speaking, one should include Belize and Panama in this group.

Table 1—Continued
Indices of development: Central American countries

Indices	Costa Rica	El Salvador	Guat- emala	Hond- uras	Nicar- agua
10. External public debt outstanding in millions of $ (1981)	2,246	664	684	1,223	1,975
11. Foreign exchange reserves in millions of $ (May 1983)	304	117	180	113	n.a.

(Based on data in World Development Report, 1983; U.N. Monthly Bulletin of Statistics, June 1983; International Financial Statistics, July 1983; Swedish International Peace Research Institute Handbook, 1983.)

Table 2
U.S. aid to Central American countries (in millions of $)

Type of aid and period	Costa Rica	El Salvador	Guat- emala	Hond- uras	Nicar- agua	Total
Economic aid						
1962-80	162	244	216	259	294	1,468*
1981	13	105	17	36	60	242*
1982	51	190	14	79	6	340
1983	215	229	37	96	neg	577
1984 (Reg)	105	294	64	83	neg	546
Totals, 1962-84	546	1,062	348	553	360	3,173
Military aid						
1962-80	3	20	40	31	31	125
1981	neg	36	neg	9	nil	45
1982	2	80	neg	31	nil	113
1983	3	110	neg	37	nil	150
1984 (Reg)	2	85	10	40	nil	137
Totals, 1962-84	10	331	50	148	31	570

(Based on data in U.S. Statistical Abstract, 1982-83, and supplied by the U.S. State Department.)

Notes: Nicaragua received $0.3 million worth of agricultural commodities through private voluntary organizations.

*Includes regional program assistance of $293 million during 1962-80 and $11 million in 1981.

"We find ourselves today on the threshold of another gigantic aid program that is almost certain, if adopted, to disappoint America's hopes."

A Marshall Plan Cannot Work

Jeffrey E. Garten

Jeffrey E. Garten was the deputy director of the State Department's Policy Planning Staff from 1978 to 1979. He is presently a vice president of Lehman Brothers, Kuhn, Loeb, Inc. In the following viewpoint, Mr. Garten attacks advocates of a Marshall Plan for Central America. He explains why he believes that what worked for Europe after World War II would fail in Central America today.

As you read, consider the following questions:

1. According to the author, why was the Marshall Plan effective in Europe following World War II?
2. Why was the Alliance for Progress a failure, according to Mr. Garten?
3. What flaws does the author believe exist in the recommendations of the Kissinger Commission?
4. What does the author recommend for Central America?

Jeffrey E. Garten, "Aid in the Eighties," *The New York Times*, March 25, 1984. Copyright © 1983/84 by The New York Times Company. Reprinted by permission.

The deeper we step into the Central American quagmire, the harder we try to keep from sinking. As military victory eludes the American-backed forces in the area, the temptation to expand economic aid becomes ever more compelling. No wonder that there have recently been calls for a Marshall Plan for the region. No wonder that the National Bipartisan Commission on Central America, headed by the former Secretary of State Henry A. Kissinger, has recommended an $8 billion aid program of economic assistance for the area over the next five years, and that the proposal has been endorsed by the Reagan Administration, as well as by many of its conservative supporters and a number of liberal newspapers and magazines.

Central America's economy is in a shambles—of that there is no doubt. But Washington's response is misguided. It is the product of the widespread American assumption that because the Marshall Plan was successful in rebuilding war-ravaged Europe, a similar formula would work in the third world. Apply enough money and enough Yankee energy in countries like Korea, Vietnam, the Congo, Brazil, Chile or the Dominican Republic—so the argument goes—and you create economic progress. Economic growth will encourage democratic government and friendship toward the United States. All good things will go together.

In 30 years of experience in Asia, Africa and Latin America, these propositions have not held true. Yet the lesson has not been learned. Once again, advocates of massive economic assistance, this time to Central America, overestimate the benefits to the recipient countries and to the United States. In expending such huge sums in the expectation of counteracting leftist rebellion and nourishing democracy in countries like El Salvador, Honduras and Guatemala, we are setting ourselves up for bitter disappointment. This could lead to a political backlash among American voters and eventual abandonment of the whole region. Better to be realistic from the start.

The Plan for Europe

To see how little there is in common between the concepts of the Marshall Plan and the realities of Central America, let us recall the situation existing in Western Europe when, on June 5, 1947, Secretary of State George C. Marshall proposed the program that came to bear his name.

Europe then was a continent torn apart by war, its people hungry, its cities destroyed, its factories silent, its mines closed, its railroads idled. Soviet-inspired Communism was threatening Greece and Turkey. Yet World War II had not destroyed Europe's advanced technical base, its social cohesion or—except for Germany—its political institutions. A well-educated population had survived; skilled management and an experienced labor force remained.

213

The task undertaken by the United States was to help rebuild the factories that had already been there, to help revive a dynamic, inventive system of industrial production and commerce, and to do all this by means of projects designed and executed primarily by the Europeans themselves. The problem was to restore what had already existed, not to create a more advanced society.

Underlying the plan was the consensus on both sides of the Atlantic that the Europeans' temporary weakness invited Soviet political infiltration, if not military aggression. It was agreed that a strong Europe required the establishment of a common market to overcome the heritage of destructive national rivalries. There was no dispute over the value of human rights.

A Ludicrous Idea

It is ludicrous to suppose that a Marshall Plan, or anything else, is going to turn Central America into a Benelux (Belgium, Netherlands, Luxembourg). Without far-reaching reforms, literally only a trickle of foreign aid would trickle down to the people who need it. Most of it would only further enrich the already bloated oligarchy and would end up in Swiss banks or Miami real estate.

Pat M. Holt, *The Christian Science Monitor*, August 3, 1983.

In these conditions, the $13 billion in aid expended by the United States produced spectacular results. By 1950, Europe's economic output far surpassed 1938 levels. Overall industrial production was up by 25 percent; steel was up by 70 percent, agriculture by 30 percent. Economic growth led to human advancement. European governments proceeded to build social-welfare systems that surpassed anything they had before the war. Political stability was strengthened. Cooperative arrangements developed in coal and steel, agriculture, labor policies and tariffs. . . .

The Alliance for Progress

President John F. Kennedy took the Marshall Plan as his inspiration for an attempt to remake Latin America under the rubric of the Alliance for Progress. The Alliance was designed in Washington at the height of the cold war. Fidel Castro had just come to power in Cuba. The third world was seen as the next battleground in the confrontation with the Soviet Union. . . .

The heart of the Alliance for Progress was social reform: the breakup of large land holdings and their redistribution among the peasants; the establishment of fair wages and good working conditions; eradication of illiteracy and disease. Much of this was to be accomplished by an infusion of $20 billion in aid from outside the region, half of it to come directly from the United States, and the rest from Western European Governments and international institutions such as the Inter-American Development Bank and the World Bank.

The results were disappointing. Economic growth did not trickle down. Some estimates showed that for each $100 per capita increase in income during the 1960's, the increase for the poorest 20 percent of the population was only $2. If you walked through the slums of Lima, Peru, or the shanty towns around Kingston, Jamaica, or the squalid countryside of northeast Brazil, you did not see any evidence that a vast regional aid program was under way.

Tax reform—indispensable to the whole concept—remained modest. Debt increased. Unemployment stayed high. And our expectations of progress toward democracy were unfulfilled. Mr. Kennedy was slow to admit that. Thus, in a 1961 speech he said: "Seven years ago there were 15 strongmen in Latin America. Today there are only five. Three years from now there won't be any." His prediction was not borne out. From 1962 to 1964, the heyday of the Alliance, there were military coups in Peru, Guatemala, Argentina and Brazil. . . .

By the end of the 1960's, it should have been clear why the success of the Marshall Plan could not be duplicated in Latin America. In Europe, we had lent a hand in reconstructing an old order; in Latin America, we tried to create a new one. In Europe, we made no pretenses about making a social revolution; south of the Rio Grande, we thought we could start a revolution and keep it under control. . . .

History Repeats Itself

What is there about 10-year cycles? A decade after the Marshall Plan, the United States undertook the Alliance for Progress. A similar period separates the end of the Alliance from the current preoccupation with Central America.

The idea of a major aid program for this region took root early in the Reagan Administration, when the fighting in El Salvador heated up and the Sandinista regime in Nicaragua accelerated its supply of arms to the Salvadoran insurgents. At first there was the Caribbean Basin Initiative, a plan for increased economic aid, tariff concessions for Central American exports to the United States, and tax write-offs for American firms investing in that area. In words recalling Mr. Kennedy's, President Reagan promised to attack the underlying causes of economic stagnation and to promote "lasting political and social tranquility based on freedom and justice."

215

As the proposal wound its way through Congress, the Administration came to be concerned that the help would be inadequate. Wishing to generate political support for more dramatic initiatives for dealing with both the security and economic dimensions of the Central American problem, the Administration established a bipartisan Presidential commission on Central America, naming Mr. Kissinger as chairman.

The commission's report last January painted a stark picture of Central America. High inflation, mounting unemployment, declining incomes, shrinking trade, capital flight, the exodus of skilled managers, a mushrooming foreign debt—these were only a few of the problems cited. According to the report, it would take $24 billion in foreign aid between now and 1990 to restore living standards to the 1980 levels. Favoring such an effort, the commission recommended an outlay of some $8 billion by the United States, more than doubling the current rate of American aid. The rest of the money would come from Europe, Japan and international organizations like the International Monetary Fund and the World Bank. For comparison, foreign aid for the region from all sources during the 18 years between 1962 and 1980 totaled about $6 billion.

The sums proposed by the Kissinger Commission were to be spent in a variety of ways: to finance critical imports, pay foreign debts, supplement investment programs, support agricultural cooperatives, broaden land ownership, stimulate small businesses, encourage private investment, build schools and houses, strengthen universities and judicial systems, and so on. . . .

In other words, the commission had returned to the concept of the Alliance for Progress—reconstruction plus social engineering—and on an even more ambitious scale. . . .

Thus, we find ourselves today on the threshold of another gigantic aid program that is almost certain, if adopted, to disappoint America's hopes. The problems of Central America are even more difficult than those for which the Alliance for Progress was designed, . . .

The Commission's Flaw

The conceptual flaw of the Alliance for Progress returns to expose a basic contradiction in the Kissinger Commission's report. If economic growth is supposed to give birth to peace, democracy and rising living standards, why didn't this happen between 1960 and 1978, when Central America enjoyed the fastest growth in its history? It was during the economic boom of the late 1970's that civil conflict flared in El Salvador, Nicaragua and Guatemala, and military governments tightened their grip on those countries and on Honduras. It was during this period of economic growth that living conditions deteriorated.

Between 1950 and 1978, per capita income doubled in the region, yet income distribution and basic living conditions worsened. By 1978, 66 percent of El Salvador's national income went to the richest 20 percent, and 2 percent went to the poorest 20 percent. In Honduras, 57 percent of the population lived in extreme poverty. In Guatemala, poor families were worse off in 1980 than they had been a decade earlier.

By 1980, despite a decade of high export earnings, major loans from foreign banks and substantial foreign aid, more than a third of the region's population could not afford an adequate diet. Ten percent of all babies below the age of 5 were dying, and 50 percent of all children were undernourished.

Should we not recognize, on the basis of this record, that there are sharp limits to what can be achieved in Central America, no matter how much aid is poured in? . . .

An Alternative Approach

The lessons of the past and the realities of Central America all argue against a massive aid program for the region. Yet for the United States to throw up its hands and walk away would be a tragic mistake. There is a middle course.

The Kissinger Commission was right in saying that the current aid levels are too low. They should be increased, but slowly, timed to the region's ability to absorb new funds. Moreover, if the Administration's aim is to boost Central America's economies for the longer run, and not simply to provide Band-Aids, United States aid should be dispensed in conjunction with economic reforms. Judgments about what constitutes adequate reform would be best left to agencies such as the International Monetary Fund or the World Bank, where short-term political considerations take a back seat to technical expertise.

In addition to aid, far more emphasis should be placed on trade. The Kissinger Commission gives lip service to removing this country's barriers against Central American exports; yet better access to the United States market would be the best and most lasting way for those nations to earn the foreign exchange they need so badly. We could start by increasing our imports of sugar, textiles and leather goods, products of exceptional value to Central America.

Of course, trade liberalization is not popular in the United States today. But better to compensate those American producers who would be hurt by increased imports than to put the money directly into Central America. This way, benefits would accrue both to American consumers, who would reap lower prices, and to the countries we are trying to help.

Central America's oppressive debt, now running at nearly $15 billion, could also be reduced. Why pour in American dollars, only to see them recycled to the United States Treasury, or, in many cases, back to Chase Manhatten or Bank of America? Here, creditors could take a leaf out of the Marshall Plan book and write off the debt.

The advantages of increasing trade and reducing debt would be far-reaching: fewer administrative burdens on Central America, funds made available without political strings, and money available for economic growth. But even a balanced aid program of this sort—moderate levels of aid, greater export opportunities, and substantial debt relief—will not work miracles. Above all, we need to deflate our expectations of economic aid as a means of promoting new democracies, decent standards of living and political stability. Central America in 1984 is not the Europe of 1948. All good things do not go together. Do we have to learn that the hard way?

Distinguishing Primary from Secondary Sources

A critical thinker must always question his or her source of knowledge. One way to critically evaluate information is to be able to distinguish between *primary sources* (a "firsthand" or eyewitness account from personal letters, documents, or speeches, etc.) and *secondary sources* (a "secondhand" account usually based upon a "firsthand" account and possibly appearing in newspapers, encyclopedias, or other similar types of publications). A diary about the Civil War written by a Civil War veteran is an example of a primary source. A history of the Civil War written many years after the war and relying, in part, upon that diary for information is an example of a secondary source.

However, it must be noted that interpretation and/or point of view also play a role when dealing with primary and secondary sources. For example, the historian writing about the Civil War not only will quote from the veteran's diary but also will interpret it. It is certainly a possibility that his or her interpretation may be incorrect. Even the diary or primary source must be questioned as to interpretation and point of view. The veteran may have been a militarist who stressed the glory of warfare rather than the human suffering involved.

This activity is designed to test your skill in evaluating sources of information. Pretend that you are writing a research paper on contemporary Central America. You decide to include an equal number of primary and secondary sources. Listed below are a number of sources which may be useful in your research. Carefully evaluate each of them. First, place a *P* next to those descriptions you feel would serve as primary sources. Second, rank the primary sources assigning the number (1) to the most objective and accurate primary source, number (2) to the next accurate and so on until the ranking is finished. Repeat the entire procedure, this time placing an *S* next to those descriptions you feel would serve as secondary sources and then ranking them.

If you are doing this activity as a member of a class or group, discuss and compare your evaluation with other members of the group. If you are reading this book alone, you may want to ask others if they agree with your evaluation. Either way, you will find the interaction very valuable.

_____ 1. A report by the state department detailing Cuban involvement in Nicaragua. _____

_____ 2. A speech given by Castro in which he claims Cuba has little if any involvement in Nicaragua. _____

_____ 3. Off the record remarks made by President Reagan on the beginnings of Cuban involvement in Central America during the Kennedy administration. _____

_____ 4. A documentary film by a left-wing organization interviewing Americans on their views of US involvement in Central America. _____

_____ 5. Viewpoint 3 in this chapter. _____

_____ 6. An editorial published in a major newspaper demanding that the US stay out of El Salvador. _____

_____ 7. A Nicaraguan businessman's remarks in which he reveals his suspicions of Nicaraguan government torture. _____

_____ 8. A native Nicaraguan newspaper extolling the virtues of the new regime. _____

_____ 9. A poem by an American liberal about a Salvadoran refugee. _____

_____ 10. The State Department's White Paper on El Salvador, detailing Communist involvement. _____

_____ 11. A US newspaper's refutation of the White Paper claiming it is bogus and exaggerated. _____

_____ 12. A history of the present Central American conflict written in the year 2100. _____

_____ 13. A Latin American novelist's surreal novel depicting lives of oppressed villagers. _____

_____ 14. A biography of the Latin American novelist. _____

Periodical Bibliography

The following list of periodical articles deals with the subject matter of this chapter.

America "Nicaragua's Peace Plan," November 5, 1983.

America "Nicaragua's Revolution," December 10, 1983.

Charles J. Beirne "Return to El Salvador," *America*, October 8, 1983.

Phillip C. Clarke "Danger at Our Doorstep," *The American Legion*, December 1983.

Peter Davis "Mirror of Our Midlife Crisis," *The Nation*, January 28, 1984.

Carlos Fuentes "Force Won't Work in Nicaragua," *The New York Times*, July 24, 1983.

William LeoGrande "Slouching Toward the Quagmire," *The Nation*, January 28, 1984.

Langhorne A. Motley "Is Peace Possible in Central America?" *Department of State Bulletin*, March 1984.

Michael Novak "Why Latin America Is Poor," *The Atlantic*, March 1982.

Robert A. Rosenblatt "Massive Aid May Have Little Effect," *The Los Angeles Times*, January 12, 1984.

Wayne S. Smith "The Choice In Central America," *Christian Science Monitor*, August 24, 1983.

Fritz Thomas "In Central America, Terminology Is Not Just Academic," *The Wall Street Journal*, April 20, 1984.

US News & World Report "It Is Not too Late for U.S. to Win in El Salvador," interview with General Nutting, June 13, 1983.

Margaret D. Wilde "What Good Would It Do to Stop the War?" *The Christian Century*, May 2, 1984.

Tom Wicker "Reagan's Big Stick," *The New York Times*, July 26, 1983.

Chronology of Events

1812	Constitutional monarchy established in Spain; colonial rule liberalized. Election of town councils in Central America marks beginning of national political life.
1814	Fernando VII restored to Spanish throne; annuls 1812 constitution and all its outgrowths in the New World.
1822	Central American provinces annex themselves to independent Mexican Empire under General Augustín de Iturbide, later Emperor Augustín I.
1823-24	Augustín I overthrown; Mexico becomes a republic. Costa Rica, Guatemala, Honduras, Nicaragua, and El Salvador form Central Federation, with capital in Guatemala City (later, briefly, San Salvador).
1825	United States and Central American Federation sign treaty of friendship, ratified following year.
1829-38	Political conflict between federation members and the capital increases. In 1838, Central American Congress allows states to leave federation; Nicaragua, Honduras and Costa Rica secede.
1847	Guatemala declares itself a "republic" rather than a "state," foreclosing possibility of reunion. Other Central American states follow suit.
1850-55	Trans-Panama railway built. Most Central American commerce moved from Caribbean to Pacific ports.
1895-99	Major efforts to restore Central American Federation fail.
1903	**Panama** declares independence from Colombia; United States quickly recognizes it and negotiates favorable treaty to build interoceanic canal.
1909	Dictator José Santos Zelaya overthrown in Nicaragua. Chaos and instability follow, leading to U.S. financial and military intervention (1911-33).
1914	**Panama Canal** opened.
1917	**Attempted Union** of five Central American states, on Honduran initiative, fails when Nicaragua refuses to cooperate.
1927	Peace accord among fighting factions in **Nicaragua** provides basis for U.S. occupation and subsequent elections. General Augusto C. Sandino refuses to accept peace accord and leads guerrilla force against U.S. Marines.

1932	Marxist-inspired uprising by peasants and Indians in El Salvador quelled by General Maximiliano Hernández Martínez. Approximately 20,000 peasants massacred in revolt against landed elite. Martinez continues repressive rule for over a decade. Military regimes follow until 1979.
1933	General Anastasio Somoza García named director of new "non-partisan" National Guard in Nicaragua. U.S. Marines withdrawn.
1927-34	General Augusto C. **Sandino** leads Nicaraguan guerrillas against U.S. occupation.
1934	**Sandino** murdered by members of Nicaraguan National Guard; Guard chief Anastasio **Somoza** dominates country until 1956.
1936	U.S.—**Panama** Canal Treaty abrogated; United States abandons protectorate powers over Panama and agrees to nonintervention.
1937	Somoza officially becomes president of Nicaragua.
1944	Dictator Jorge Ubico in **Guatemala** resigns under pressure of violence and protests.
1944-50	"Spiritual socialist" Juan José Arévalo heads reformist administration in **Guatemala.**
1948	**Fraudulent conservative government in Costa Rica** overthrown by José Figueres and his Army of National Liberation; start of long period of democratic institutions and dominance of Figueres in Costa Rican politics.
1948	**Organization of American States** (OAS) created.
1950-54	Jacobo Arbenz elected president of **Guatemala.** Revolutionary reforms intensify; Communist infiltration of government increases.
1952	Fulgencio Batista seizes power in **Cuba** and establishes repressive dictatorship.
1953	Cuban revolutionary leader Fidel **Castro** imprisoned after unsuccessful attack on army post in Santiago de Cuba.
1954	OAS "Declaration of Solidarity" against intervention of International Communism is directed against Arbenz government in **Guatemala.** After Eastern European arms arrive, Colonel Carlos Castillo Armas overthrows Arbenz with aid of Honduras, Nicaragua and U.S.
1955	Fidel Castro released from Cuban prison; goes to Mexico.
1956	**Somoza** assassinated; sons Luis and Anastasio Jr. continue family domination of Nicaragua to 1979.

1956	Fidel **Castro** and several dozen companions arrive in Cuba from Mexico to begin guerrilla struggle.
1957	Castillo Armas assassinated. Period of instability and violence begins in **Guatemala.**
1958-63	Conservative Miguel Ydígoras Fuentes elected president of **Guatemala.**
1961	Sandinista National Liberation Front (FSLN) founded in Nicaragua.
1961	US.-sponsored exile invasion of **Cuba** fails to establish beachhead at Bay of Pigs; Castro declares himself Marxist-Leninist and ally of Soviet Union.
1962	U.S.-Soviet crisis over placement of strategic missiles in **Cuba** resolved by compromise: Soviet Union agrees to remove the weapons; U.S. promises not to invade the island.
1964	Riots in **Panama Canal Zone** lead to new canal treaty negotiations.
1965	U.S. intervention in **Dominican Republic** restores order after leftwing insurgency.
1967	Anastasio Somoza Debayle elected president in Nicaragua.
1969	"Soccer War" over border tensions with Honduras. Honduran president Colonel Fidel Sánchez Hernández expels 300,000 illegal Salvadoran immigrants.
1972	Earthquake devastates Managua, **Nicaragua**; Somoza's mishandling of crisis and of international relief funds increases antipathy to regime.
1972	Christian Democrat José Napoleón Duarte wins plurality in presidential election in El Salvador. Legislature, however, acting within constitution chooses Colonel Arturo Armando Molina as president. Duarte charges fraud, is arrested and exiled.
1972	Michael Manley of pro-socialist People's National Party begins first term as prime minister of **Jamaica**.
1974	Election fraud ensures Somoza's reelection to six-year term in **Nicaragua.**
1977	Popular unrest intensifies in Nicaragua. U.S. suspends credits to Somoza government through votes at World Bank and Inter-American Development Bank.
1977	New Panama Canal treaties establishing means for eventually ceding canal to **Panama** ratified by U.S. Senate after long fight.
1978	U.S. and Organization of American States fail in mediation attempts with Nicaragua; U.S. suspends military aid to Somoza.

1979	Somoza overthrown in **Nicaragua;** new governing coalition dominated by marxist FSLN (Sandinista Liberation Front) assumes power.
1979	Young military officers overthrow **El Salvador** dictator General Carlos Humberto Romero.
1979	Maurice Bishop seizes control of **Grenada** while elected prime minister Eric Gairy is out of country.
1980	New government of **El Salvador** declares land, tax and banking reforms. Carter administration suspends U.S. aid to Nicaragua because of evidence that FSLN is arming Salvadoran insurgents. In December, José Napoleón Duarte becomes president of military-civilian junta.
1980	Archbishop Oscar Arnulfo Romero assassinated while saying Mass in El Salvador by unknown gunman.
1980	Revolutionary Democratic Front (FDR), a rebel political arm, formed. Guerrilla umbrella organization, Farabundo Martí National Liberation Front (FMLN), created with help of Fidel Castro. Three strikes called by rebels in summer fail.
1980	Four American churchwomen in El Salvador murdered; in response, President Carter suspends economic aid to government.
1981	President Carter lifts arms embargo begun four years earlier in El Salvador.
1981	Rebel forces in El Salvador launch "final offensive" to present U.S. president-elect Reagan with *fait accompli*; fails through lack of popular support.
1981	U.S. Congress requires semi-annual certification of progress in human rights in **El Salvador** as condition for military aid.
1981	Anti-Communist **Jamaica** Labor Party defeats Michael Manley; Edward Seaga becomes prime minister.
1982	Elections held in **El Salvador** under Duarte for Constituent Assembly. Large voter turnout despite boycott, threats, and violence by rebels. Alvaro Magaña named provisional president; is first elected civilian head of government in fifty years.
1982	President Reagan launches **Caribbean Basin Initiative.**
1983	Marxist dictator Maurice Bishop and other group government officials in **Grenada** murdered in October by hard-line Marxists led by Bernard Coard. U.S. forces invade Grenada to restore peace and parliamentary democracy; Coard imprisoned, Cuban "advisors" expelled.

1983	US military adviser Albert Arthur Schaufelberger assassinated in El Salvador.
1983	Reagan increases military excercises off Nicaragua.
1983	George Shultz demands end to Death Squad activity in El Salvador by January 10, 1984 for continued US aid.
1984	The Kissinger Commission releases its report; recommends more economic and military aid to Central America.
1984	Congress gives the go-ahead for more US aid to El Salvador.
1984	CIA mines Nicaraguan harbor. World Court finds US violating international law.
1984	Four guerrilla guardsmen convicted of the murders of four church-women in El Salvador.
1984	José Napoleon Duarte elected president of El Salvador in free elections.

Reprinted with permission from *Crisis and Opportunity: U.S. Policy in Central America and the Caribbean*, edited by Mark Falcoff and Robert Royal, published by the Ethics and Public Policy Center, 1030 15th Street NW, Washington DC 20005.

Glossary of Terms

agrarian reform Plan to redistribute land from the landowners to the landless peasants and *campesinos.*

Alliance for Progress Adopted in 1961 by the Kennedy Administration to provide economic aid to Central America. Its proposed objectives were redistribution of land and tax reforms. Coming on the heels of the Castro takeover of Cuba, it was meant to discourage Communism by providing prosperity.

CADO (Central America Development Organization) Proposed by the Kissinger Commission. Members would include Belize, Costa Rica, El Salvador, Guatemala, Honduras, Nicaragua, Panama and the US. Organized to promote regional development, political pluralism, elections and economic reconstruction.

campesino Rural farm peasant.

Caribbean Basin Initiative (CBI) Proposed by the Reagan Administration and passed by Congress in January 1984, meant to promote economic growth and political stability in Central America and the Caribbean. Components include giving 28 nations economic assistance and duty-free access to US markets for 12 years. Also proposes military aid to the nations of Central America.

CIA (Central Intelligence Agency) US intelligence organization involved in training Salvadoran *contras* and implicated in the mining of the Nicaraguan harbors.

CONDECA (*Consejo de Defensa Centroamericano*) Central American Defense Council; set up by the US as a regional counterinsurgency force coordinated by the military heads of El Salvador, Honduras, Guatemala and Nicaragua. After the fall of Somoza, CONDECA virtually fell apart as an alliance, despite US attempts to revive it within Guatemala.

Contadora group Comprising four countries: Colombia, Mexico, Panama and Venezuela. The group presented a document to the United Nations proposing its objectives on October 6, 1983, in which they formulated a non-interventionist stance. The US opposed their proposals while the international community supported them.

contra US-backed forces opposing the Nicaraguan government. Reagan calls "freedom fighters." Others, who oppose them, label them "Somocistas," because they feel the *contras* are dissatisfied backers of Somoza.

COSEP (*Consejo Superior de la Empresa Privada*) Higher Council of Private Enterprise. The Nicaraguan Businessman's Association. Critical of the Sandinista government.

counterinsurgency Organized military activity designed to oppose revolt against government in power.

counterrevolutionary Organized military group opposing revolutionary element or government.

despotism Government in which the ruler has unlimited power.

EGP (Ejército Guerrillero De Los Pobres) Poor People's Guerrilla Army of Guatemala. This communist-inspired guerrilla group is comprised mostly of Guatemalan Indians and is one of the largest and most organized.

estación de muertes Spanish term for right-wing death squads of El Salvador.

FD (*Frente Democrático*) The Democratic Front of El Salvador is a group of three organizations: MPSC, the Popular Social Christian Movement, a group of dissident Democratic Christians; MNR, Revolutionary National Movement; and MIPTES, Independent Movement of Professionals and Technicians.

FDR (*Frente Democrático Revolucionário*) The Revolutionary Democratic Front. The Political arm of leftist Salvadoran opposition in El Salvador.

FMLN (*Farabúndo Martí*) An umbrella term for the National Liberation Front, the five guerilla factions in El Salvador.

FPL (*Fuerzas Populares de Liberación*) The Popular Liberation Forces of El Salvador, founded in 1970, the oldest guerrilla faction.

FSLN (*Frente Sandinista de Liberación Nacional*) Sandinist National Liberation of Nicaragua. Led the organized opposition to Somoza.

guerrillas Those who engage in irregular warfare. The guerrillan forces overthrew and replaced Somoza in Nicaragua.

imperialism Extending the power and influence of a nation by direct territorial acquisitions or by gaining indirect control over the political or economic life of other areas.

indigenous Native, originating in said country. Used primarily to distinguish a native revolution from one that is influenced from outside political and social pressures. The Nicaraguan and El Salvadoran revolutions are often debated in this context.

insurrection Revolt against civil authority or an established government.

junta Council for political or governmental purposes. In Central America, junta mostly refers to organized military opposition.

Kissinger Commission Assembled by Ronald Reagan in 1983 and formally titled The National Bipartisan Commission on Central America it is most often referred to as the Kissinger Commission because of its controversial chairman, Henry Kissinger. It issued its report in January 1984 recommending increases in economic and military aid. With Kissinger abstaining, the report also recommended that this aid be incumbent upon improvement in human rights.

La Prensa National newspaper of Nicaragua. The newspaper has become a barometer of Nicaraguan revolutions. *La Prensa*'s editor, Pedro Joaquín Chamorro, was murdered by the Somoza National Guard. The paper is also critical of the Sandinistan regime and consequently the Sandinistas have also come under attack for periodically shutting down and censoring the paper.

left-wing Term to describe Central American revolutionaries and opposers to dictatorships.

Marshall Plan Program to foster economic recovery in certain European countries after World War II. George C. Marshall called upon European countries to make recommendations of their needs so that material and financial aid from the United States could begin on a broad scale. It was completed in 1952. Reagan's massive economic aid program to Central America is often called the new Marshall Plan.

Marxist-Leninist Followers of the Karl Marx/Vladimir Lenin type of socialism communism. Also used in a negative way to describe the Nicaraguan Sandinist government.

Monroe Doctrine Accredited to President James Monroe, the doctrine originally stated that the US would not tolerate European intervention or colonization in the Americas. Roosevelt added that continued disturbance in Latin America might be grounds for US intervention.

National Guard US-supported Nicaraguan occupation force headed by Anastasio Somoza. Responsible for many documented violent acts committed against Nicaraguan people who were suspected of Communist activity.

OAS (Organization of American States) International organization that compiles an annual Human Rights Report. It called for the resignation of Somoza and opposed US intervention in Nicaragua. In 1978, after documenting numerous human rights violations, it condemned the Salvadoran government as well.

OLAS (Latin American Solidarity Organization) Group that is headquartered in Havana and supportive of Latin American revolution.

ORDEN (*Organización Democrática Nacionalista*) Democratic Nationalist Organization; has been called the "gestapo" of El Salvador. Begun in the 1960s, it was composed of spies, government loyalists and peasants who were recruited and paid by the National Guard to keep track of potential "subversives" in their respective communities.

ORPA (Organazación Pueblo en Armas) People in Arms Organization, large communist-inspired guerrilla organization of Guatemala. Its members are mostly Indian.

oligarchy A government in which a small group maintains control for corrupt and selfish purposes.

paramilitary An auxillary military force.

power-sharing Proposed by the FMLN/FDR guerrilla organizations of El Salvador to seek participation in an interim government along with the established government to help achieve elections. Power-sharing was rejected by the US.

right-wing Supporters of the Central American dictatorships, usually conservative landowners and businessmen. The National Guard of Nicaragua was described as a right-wing organization.

Sandinism Sandinist philosophy, which, according to the Sandinistas themselves, combines both the philosophy of Karl Marx and elements of Christianity.

Sandinista Revolutionary guerrillas and followers of General Sandino who overthrew Somoza on July 19, 1979. The Sandinistas head the present Nicaraguan government.

Sandino, César Augusto A guerrilla leader, he began fighting the US Marine occupation force in 1927 and continued fighting successfully until their withdrawal in 1933. US-trained National Guard leader Anastasio Somoza assasinated Sandino, overthrew the liberal president Juan Sacassa and established a military dictatorship.

Somocista Supporters of General Anastasio Somoza. Also used to describe members of the US-supported *contras*.

Somoza family The Somoza family dominated Nicaragua from 1937-1979. All of the Somozas received US support. The final dictator of Nicaragua, Anastasio Debayle, ruled from 1967-1979, until the Sandinista takeover. He is well-known for his repressive government and extreme human rights violations.

White Paper on El Salvador State Department report issued in 1981. In sum, the report justified US military involvement by citing communist military support in the area. It was later discredited by major US newspapers, and the State Department admitted some of its statistics were based on "guesses."

Organizations to Contact

American Enterprise Institute for Policy Research
1150 17th St. NW
Washington, DC 20036
(202) 862-5800

The institute is a conservative think tank that researches a number of issues, including foreign policy and defense.

American Friends Service Committee
1501 Cherry St.
Philadelphia, PA 19102
(215) 241-7000

The AFSC is a Quaker organization that believes in the dignity and worth of every person and that the US should stop financing anti-Sandinista groups, stop forcing Honduras and Costa Rica to oppose Nicaragua, and give genuine support to the initiatives of the Contadora group and others.

Americas Watch Committee
205 E. 42nd St. Rm 1303
New York, NY 10017
(212) 840-9460

The organization is dedicated to monitoring and promoting observance of human rights in the Western Hemisphere. It publishes a variety of reports on the world human rights situation, including Central America. Write for a list of publications.

Cardinal Mindszenty Foundation
PO Box 11321
St. Louis, MO 63105
(314) 991-2939

This anti-communist organization was founded in 1958 to conduct educational and research activities concerning communist objectives, tactics and propaganda through study groups, speakers, conferences and films. It publishes the monthly *Mindszenty Report*.

Center for Defense Information
303 Capitol Gallery West
600 Maryland Ave. SW
Washington, DC 20024
(202) 484-9490

The Center for Defense Information supports a strong defense but opposes excessive expenditures for weapons and policies that increase the danger of nuclear war. It believes that strong social, economic and political structures contribute equally to national security and are essential to the strength and welfare of our country.

Center for International Policy
120 Maryland Ave. NE
Washington, DC 20002
(202) 544-4666

The Center is an education and research organization concerned with US foreign policy towards the Third World and its impact on human rights and human needs.

Center for Philosophy and Public Policy
College Park, Maryland 20742
(301) 454-4103

The Center examines topics expected to be important issues of public policy debate over the next decade. The research is conducted cooperatively by interdisciplinary working groups composed of philosophers, policymakers and analysts. This diversity permits comprehensive examination of the major aspects of the complex issues investigated.

Central America Resource Center
1701 University Ave. SE
Minneapolis, MN 55414
(612) 379-8799

The Center is an organization dedicated to justice for the people of Central America. They support their right to determine their own future, and they recognize the need for fundamental economic, political and social change. They believe US policy must be changed to one which respects the basic rights and needs of the Central American people.

Citizens Committee on the El Salvador Crisis
2211 Broadway, Suite 7G
New York, NY 10024
(212) 724-0371

The Committee believes that the majority of El Salvadorans desire reform, democratic elections and a political solution to the current conflict and believes that US troops should not intervene. It publishes pamphlets and press releases.

Clergy and Laity Concerned
198 Broadway
New York, NY 10038
(212) 964-6730

A group concerned with human rights and racial justice, they publish a monthly newsletter, *CALC Report*, that focuses on a number of political issues.

Coalition for a New Foreign and Military Policy
120 Maryland Ave. NE
Washington, DC 20002
(202) 546-8400

The Coalition works for a peaceful, non-interventionist and demilitarized US foreign policy. It wants to reduce military spending, protect human rights and promote arms control and disarmament. A subscription to *Coalition Close-Up* published quarterly, and other publications, is included in its annual $20 membership fee.

Commission on United States-Central American Relations
1826 18th St. NW
Washington, DC 20009
(202) 483-0022

The Commission was created out of a deep concern about the current course of American policy toward the countries of the Caribbean region. Their purpose is to focus public attention upon crucial issues in American policy toward Central America, provide reliable assessments of the impact of our policies there, and produce alternatives that can be debated and adopted by public officials.

Council for the Defense of Freedom
P.O. Box 28526
Washington, DC 20005

The Council is concerned about the mortal danger the US will face if it does not stop communist aggression. Its weekly paper, *The Washington Inquirer,* repeatedly deals with the arms race and US failure to take measures to overcome a lack of preparedness.

Department of Defense
Office of Public Affairs
Public Correspondence Division
Room 2E 777
Washington, DC 20037

Write for a list of publications and an order form.

El Salvador Research and Information Center
PO Box 4797
Berkeley, CA 94704
(415) 843-5041

The Center is dedicated to the study of US relations with El Salvador and Central America. Its objective is to contribute to the public understanding of the situation through publications and projects.

Ethics and Public Policy Center
1030 15th St. NW
Washington, DC 20005
(202) 682-1200

The Center was founded to clarify and reinforce the bond between the Judeo-Christian moral tradition and domestic and foreign policy issues. The Center publishes original essays and reprints.

The Heritage Foundation
214 Massachusetts Ave. NE
Washington, DC 20002
(202) 546-4400

The foundation is dedicated to limited government, individual and economic freedom and a strong national defense. It supports US involvement in Central America to stop communist influence in the area.

Humanitas/International
P.O. Box 818
Menlo Park, CA 94026
(415) 324-9077

A non-partisan organization founded and administered by folksinger Joan Baez. It identifies and assists victims of human rights violations. It believes that a respect for human rights is essential for a preservation of human dignity. The organization publishes a quarterly newsletter, *Humanitas International*.

Inter-American Commission on Human Rights
Organization of American States
1889 F St. NW
Washington, DC 20006
(202) 789-6000

The Organization serves to promote cooperation among the American Republics and is a regional agency of the United Nations. The Commission's principal function is to promote the observance and protection of human rights. It monitors the human rights situation in the member-countries by examining denounced violations, on-site inspections and other procedures. They publish documents that are available upon request.

Nicaraguan Embassy
1627 New Hampshire Ave. NW
Washington, DC 20009
(202) 387-4371

The embassy is against US covert activity in Nicaragua and unflinchingly defends its sovereignty, independence and territorial integrity.

North American Congress on Latin America, Inc.
151 West 19th St.
New York, NY 10011
(212) 989-8890

The Congress is an independent research organization founded to document US corporate, military and political activities in Latin America and to relate those to conditions in the US. It publishes an influential bimonthly newsletter that focuses on Central America, *Report on the Americas*, and pamphlets and books.

Overview Latin America
9 Sacramento St.
Cambridge, MA 02138
(617) 354-0576

This human rights education group is dedicated to uncovering the social, political and economic roots of poverty and repression in Latin America. It mobilizes support and lobbies for US government policies for Latin America and publishes a variety of publications.

Religious Task Force on Central America
1747 Connecticut Ave. NW
Washington, DC 20009
(202) 387-7652

The task forces's objectives are to stop US intervention in and aid to Central America and to educate people about circumstances there. It publishes a variety of newsletters and reports.

Unitarian Universalist Service Committee
78 Beacon St.
Boston, MA 02108
(617) 742-2120

The Committee is dedicated to promoting economic, social, civil and political rights of people throughout the world. It opposes US intervention in Central America.

US Committee in Solidarity with the People of El Salvador (CISPES)
P.O. Box 12066
Washington, DC 20005
(202) 887-5019

The committee supports self-determination for Salvadorans and seeks a halt to US intervention in El Salvador. It publishes a monthly newsletter.

Washington Office on Latin America
110 Maryland Ave. NE
Washington, DC 20002
(202) 544-8045

The Washington Office on Latin America seeks to encourage US policies which promote human rights and to strengthen democratic trends in Latin America. It is committed to the belief that 1) the US and Latin America are tied by geography and history; 2) that US policy has a great impact on Latin America and 3) that the American public wants to know about and supports US policies which are conducive to the betterment of all peoples who live in Latin America. It publishes a monthly newsletter.

Bibliography of Books

Robert Armstrong and Janet Shenk — *El Salvador: The Face of Revolution,* Boston: South End Press, 1982.

Phillip Berryman — *The Religious Roots of Rebellion,* Maryknoll: New York, 1984.

Phillip Berryman — *What's Wrong in Central America and What To Do About It,* Philadelphia: American Friends Service Committee, 1983.

Cole Blasier — *The Giant's Rival: The U.S.S.R. in Latin America,* U of Pittsburgh Press, 1983.

John A. Booth — *The End and the Beginning: The Nicaraguan Revolution,* New York: Westview Press, 1982.

Bernard Diedreich — *Somoza and the Legacy of U.S. Involvement in Central America,* New York: E.P. Dutton, 1981.

Marvin Diskin — *Trouble in our Backyard,* New York: Pantheon Books, 1983.

Marlene Dixon and Susanne Jonas — *Revolution and Intervention in Central America,* San Francisco: Synthesis Publications, 1983.

Michael Erisman — *Colossus Challenged: The Caribbean Struggle for Influence,* Boulder, CO: Westview Press, 1982.

Mark Falcoff and Robert Royal — *Crisis and Opportunity, U.S. Policy in Central America and the Carribean,* Washington D.C.: Ethics and Public Policy Center, 1984.

Marvin E. Gettleman, and others — *El Salvador: Central America in the New Cold War,* New York: Grove Press, 1981.

Barry B. Levine — *The New Cuban Presence in the Caribbean,* Boulder CO: Westview Press, 1982.

Carla Anne Robbins — *The Cuban Threat,* New York: McGraw Hill Book Co, 1983.

Thomas W. Walker — *Nicaragua in Revolution,* New York: Prager, 1982.

Robert Wesson — *Communism in Central America and the Caribbean,* Stanford, CA: Hoover Institution Press, 1982.

Richard Alan White — *The Morass: United States Intervention in Central America,* New York: Harper and Row, 1984.

Index

243